WORLD WAR 2 FOR KIDS

AMAZING FACTS, EPIC BATTLES, HEROES AND VILLAINS, SECRET MISSIONS, SPIES AND CODEBREAKERS.

ALL YOU NEED TO KNOW ABOUT WW2!

JAMES BURROWS

© **Copyright 2024 - All rights reserved.**

The content contained within this book may not be reproduced, duplicated or transmitted without direct written permission from the author or the publisher.

Under no circumstances will any blame or legal responsibility be held against the publisher, or author, for any damages, reparation, or monetary loss due to the information contained within this book, either directly or indirectly.

Legal Notice:

This book is copyright protected. It is only for personal use. You cannot amend, distribute, sell, use, quote or paraphrase any part, or the content within this book, without the consent of the author or publisher.

Disclaimer Notice:

Please note the information contained within this document is for educational and entertainment purposes only. All effort has been executed to present accurate, up to date, reliable, complete information. No warranties of any kind are declared or implied. Readers acknowledge that the author is not engaged in the rendering of legal, financial, medical or professional advice. The content within this book has been derived from various sources. Please consult a licensed professional before attempting any techniques outlined in this book.

By reading this document, the reader agrees that under no circumstances is the author responsible for any losses, direct or indirect, that are incurred as a result of the use of the information contained within this document, including, but not limited to, errors, omissions, or inaccuracies.

CONTENTS

1. WELCOME TO THE BATTLEFIELD — 5
2. BIG MOMENTS & BIG NUMBERS — 9
3. HEROES AND VILLAINS — 16
4. THE BATTLE ZONES — 36
   - The Road to War — 36
   - Invasion of Poland — 37
   - The Conquest of Europe — 38
   - Britain Under Attack - The Battle of Britain — 42
   - British Cities Bombed - The Blitz — 46
   - The Siege of Leningrad — 50
   - The United States Enters the War - Pearl Harbor — 53
   - Skies Ablaze in The Pacific – The Battle of Midway — 57
   - The Battle of Stalingrad - History's Bloodiest Battle? — 60
   - Battle in North Africa's Desert – El Alamein — 63
   - Tanks Clash at Kursk — 66
   - Allied Invasion of Europe - D-Day — 70
   - Island Hopping in the Pacific – The Battle of Iwo Jima — 79
   - The Ultimate Weapon – Dropping of The Atom Bombs — 84
   - Submarine Warfare – The Battle From Under The Waves — 89
   - Battle of Berlin – the End of the War in Europe — 92
5. DARK TIMES – NAZIS AND JEWS — 99
   - Why Did the Nazis Persecute the Jews? — 100
   - Kristallnacht — 100
   - Ghettos — 101
   - Concentration Camps — 103

Anne Frank	106
The End and Aftermath	106
6. SECRET MISSIONS, SPIES AND CODE BREAKERS	110
Secret Missions	110
Spies and Resistance Fighters	115
Scientists	121
7. TECH AND GADGETS	127
Kit	127
Food	128
Weapons	129
Technology	130
Aircraft	135
8. PRISONERS OF WAR (POWS)	142
Germany	143
Japan	144
Russia	145
America	146
Britain	147
Famous POW's Prison Escapes	148
9. VICTORY CELEBRATIONS AND WHAT HAPPENED NEXT	150
Victory Celebrations	150
The United Nations	157
The Cold War	157
Conclusion	159
About the Author	161

1

WELCOME TO THE BATTLEFIELD

Hey there! Are you ready for an extraordinary journey through one of the most exciting and important chapters in history? Buckle up, because we're about to embark on an adventure through the thrilling twists and turns of World War II!

Hold on tight because we're going to explore the pages of history like never before. We'll uncover the mysteries behind epic battles, meet real-life heroes, and discover the remarkable events that shaped the world during and after World War II.

But wait - this isn't your average history lesson. Look out for our Amazing Facts throughout the book. We've sprinkled in loads of trivia, incredible war facts, some amazing, some crazy, some gruesome as well as mind-boggling facts to make learning about this crucial period as exciting as a rollercoaster ride!

AMAZING FACTS

So, whether you're a seasoned history buff or just starting your journey into the past, get ready for an adventure that will transport you to a time when the world faced its darkest times, its biggest challenges, heroes rose to the occasion and when good, conquered evil.

Grab your explorer hat, bring your curiosity, and let's jump into World War 2. The past is waiting to share its secrets, and we're about to uncover them together. Are you excited? Let's get started!

What was World War 2?

World War 2 was the biggest and deadliest war in history. It lasted for 6 six years, from 1939 to 1945 and was fought on 6 continents (who would want to fight in the freezing cold of Antarctica!).

There were 2 opposing sides –

- The Allies - including the UK, France, the USA, Soviet Union and China
- The Axis Powers - including Germany, Italy and Japan.

The Second World War started because of some of the things that happened at the end of the First World War. In 1919, the countries that were victorious in WW1 created the Treaty of Versailles that punished Germany, and lots of Germans thought they had been treated unfairly. Adolf Hitler used this feeling of unfairness, the high unemployment rate and general instability in Germany, to rise to power on promises to fix the issues facing the German people. In reality, Hitler broke international agreements, re-armed the German military, and invaded other countries.

For the other Axis countries, Japan was becoming more aggressive and militaristic and wanted to expand in Asia to gain access to raw materials. Italy was governed by a Fascist dictator who wanted to restore Italy's past glories.

There were heroes on all sides - leaders who stood up for what they believed in. But there were also appalling horrors, like the Holocaust, where innocent people suffered terribly. It was a time of incredible courage and unimaginable pain.

Eventually, in 1945, the Allies won. The war ended, but the world had changed. The United Nations was formed to keep the peace, and new superpowers emerged. The atomic bombs dropped on Hiroshima and Nagasaki in Japan, made everyone realize the destructive power of modern weapons.

World War II left a lasting mark. It showed the world the importance of working together for peace. The Nuremberg Trials held leaders accountable for war crimes, and the world promised "never again" to atrocities like the Holocaust.

So, there you have it—the whirlwind of World War II, where the stakes were high, heroes were born, and the world learned some tough lessons about the cost of conflict and the value of peace.

AMAZING FACTS

- *Soldiers from many countries fought in the war including Australia, South Africa, Canada, New Zealand and India.*
- *American was officially neutral, until the Japanese attack at Pearl Harbor.*
- *14 countries were neutral – they didn't pick a side to support or fight alongside. These included Sweden, Portugal, Spain, Ireland and Switzerland.*
- *The death rate of Russian soldiers was huge - 80% of Russian men born in 1923 were killed in WW2!*
- *Before America entered the war, Americans fought for other Allied countries even though it was illegal for them to do so. 11 Americans pilots flew in the British RAF in the Battle of Britain. In 1940, the Eagle Squadrons were formed – 6,700 Americans applied, 244 were selected.*
- *Americans also fought in the Chinese Air Force, and were known as the Flying Tigers!*
- *60,000 Americans volunteered to fight for Nazi Germany!*

2

BIG MOMENTS & BIG NUMBERS

Let's look at some of the most important moments of World War 2 and some mind-boggling numbers, that will make your eyes widen and your brain do somersaults!

September 1, 1939 - Britain and France declared war on Germany, after it invaded Poland. Germany had already invaded Austria and part of Czechoslovakia.

Summer 1940 – Germany had invaded and captured most of Europe, including Denmark, Norway, Netherlands, Belgium, Luxembourg and France. The Allies were defeated at Dunkirk, where the British were forced to retreat across The Channel. Britain now faced Hitler's Germany alone.

July – October 1940 – The Battle of Britain when Germany's air force (called the Luftwaffe) attacked Britain. The British RAF won and the attack stopped after 3 months.

September 1940 – The Blitz. For 57 nights in a row, London was bombed by the German air force (the Luftwaffe). In total, the bombing lasted for 8 months, but the British would not be beaten.

June 1941 – Operation Barbarossa, launching Germany's invasion of Russia.

September 1941 – The Siege of Leningrad, in Russia, begins in which an estimated 1.5 million people were killed or starved to death.

December 1941 – Japan bombs Pearl Harbour, in Hawaii, part of the USA. This was a huge turning point in the war, as it brought the United States into the war, when it declared war on Japan.

January 1942 – The Nazis implemented what they called 'The Final Solution' and started to kill Jews in large numbers in concentration camps.

June 1942 – The Battle of Midway, in the Pacific Ocean, a naval battle where the USA defeated the Japanese navy. From this point, Japan was on the defensive in the war.

August 1942 – The Battle of Stalingrad begins in Russia and left 2 million casualties.

July 1943 – The Battle of Kursk, the largest tank battle in history was launched by the Germans against Russia. The battle stopped the German advance on Russia and started to turn the tide of the war to the Allies.

September 1943 – Italy surrenders

June 6, 1944 – D-Day – United States, British and Canadian soldiers land in France, the largest seaborne invasion in history. This was the start of freeing Europe of the Nazis.

March 1945 – The Battle of Iwo Jima. The United States captured this island from the Japanese, which then gave the Allies a base close to Japan. Iwo Jima is 650 miles south of Tokyo.

April 20, 1945 – The Battle of Berlin begins, one of the final battles of WW2, with the Soviets attacking the city.

April 30, 1945 – Hitler kills himself.

May 7, 1945 – Germany surrenders.

May 8th, 1945 – Victory in Europe Day or VE Day with celebrations marking the official end of the war in Europe. Meanwhile, the war in the Pacific against Japan continued.

August 6, 1945 – The 1st atomic bomb was dropped on Hiroshima in Japan, by the Americans. The bomb was called Little Boy.

August 9, 1945 – The 2nd atomic bomb was dropped on Japan, this time on the city of Nagasaki. This bomb was called Fat Man.

September 2, 1945 – Japan surrenders, and the 2nd World War is finally over.

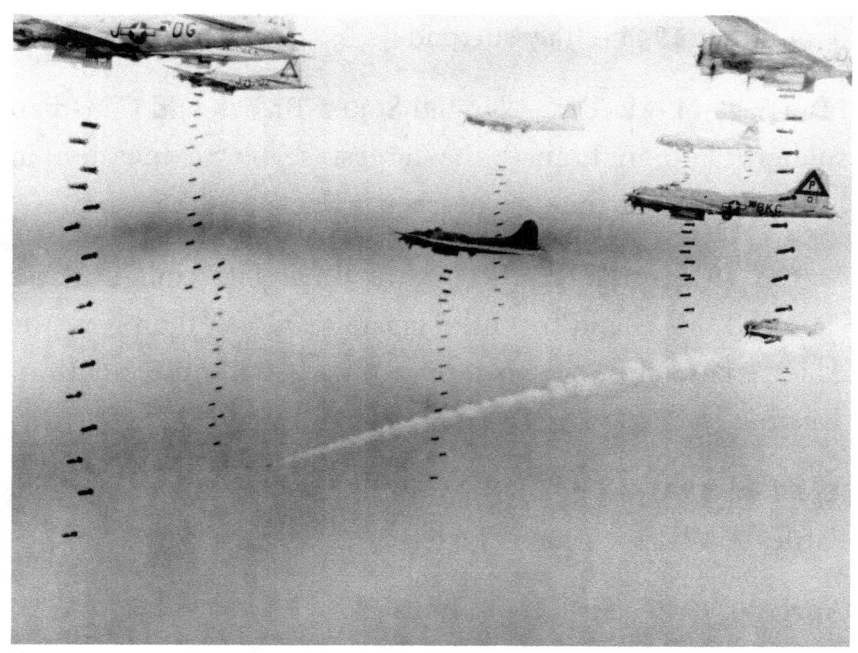

B-17 Flying Fortresses of U.S. 8th Air Force bombing Dresden, April 17, 1945.

AMAZING FACTS

Shocking numbers

The number of people who fought in the war is almost unbelievable - 127 million! That is around 5% of the world at the time. Estimates for the major countries are:

34 million – Soviet Union
18 million - Germany
16 million – United States
14 million – China
9 million – Japan
5.8 million - Britain

194 – *countries involved in the war*
15 million – *soldiers killed*
45 million – *civilians (people who are not soldiers) killed*
6 million – *the number of Jews killed by the Nazis*
16 million – *people left homeless*
41.4 billion – *bullets made by the United States, enough to take 10 shots at every person alive at the time*
297,000 – *aircraft produced by the United States*
86,000 – *tanks made by the United States*
3,000 – *Allied ships sunk by German submarines (called U-boats)*
4.5 million – *military trucks made*
$4 trillion – *total cost of the war*

U.S. soldiers operating Signal Corps radios. One man cranks the hand generator, while another uses a hand-held radio set. June 6-8, 1944, Normandy, France.

Surprising amounts!

1.5 million – the number of children in Britain evacuated from cities and sent to the countryside to live, where it was thought the children would be safer. Some children were away from their homes for 5 years and didn't recognise their parents when they returned!

3,000 - the number of babies one midwife delivered at Auschwitz concentration camp during the Holocaust

3 to 22 - the of sheets of toilet paper rationed to soldiers for each day—the British got 3, while the Americans were lucky – they got 22!

100 – the number of Japanese soldiers John McKinney fought off, by himself, using only his rifle. He killed 38 of them.

84 - the number of generals that Hitler had executed, mostly after he discovered they were plotting to kill him

1,400 - the number of missions Luftwaffe pilot Erich Hartmann flew in his Messerschmitt, with 352 kills

41 – the number of kills for Marmaduke "Pat" Prattle, a South African, the ace pilot of the RAF. He was shot down and killed in 1941.

75 hours – the longest time a German U-Boat could stay submerged, under water. Almost 3 days! Some types of U-Boat could only stay under water for 14 hours before the air ran out.

1 in 10 – *not all bombs dropped exploded - 1 in every 10 didn't! 2,000 tons of unexploded bombs are still found in Germany each year, almost 80 years after the war finished!*

U.S. infantry patrol picking its way through the ruins of Saint Lo, France. The town was 95% destroyed before it was captured from Germans on July 18, 1944

3

HEROES AND VILLAINS

During the chaos of war, heroes emerged from the courageous soldiers storming the beaches of Normandy to the daring spies weaving complex webs of deception. These were not just soldiers; they were ordinary men and women facing scary and tough situations – their strength and courage were amazing!

Yet, as heroes stood tall, villains cast their evil shadows - dark figures, causing trouble and spreading hate. These sinister regimes and leaders who sought to impose their twisted ideologies plunged the world into a war that tested humanity to its very limits.

Let's get started with our first villain - it's probably easy to guess who that is!

Adolf Hitler – Leader of Germany

Adolf Hitler was without doubt, a bad guy! Through his twisted beliefs and actions, he was responsible for the deaths of more than 17 million people! An extraordinary number that certainly puts him near the top of the worst people to have ever lived. So how did he become the leader of Germany? What did the German people see in him? To answer that, we need to go back to the end of World War 1.

Adolf Hitler

World War 1 was supposed to be the 'war to end all wars', but the punishment of Germany after the war ended and the ambition and mistrust between countries would eventually lead to the 2nd World War.

Germany had to pay 132 billion gold marks (worth $500 billion today) in damages for World War 1, its economy was in ruins, and many people were unemployed and suffered financially. Germans felt angry and frustrated and wanted someone to fix everything.

AMAZING FACTS

- *Before the war, the price of food doubled almost every four days in Germany. A loaf of bread cost 163 marks in 1922 – but 200 billion marks a year later. Eventually, even a wheelbarrow full of money couldn't buy a loaf of bread.*
- *The value of money fell so quickly that people had to be paid twice a day! This made Germans very angry and many blamed Britain and America for their problems.*
- *It took 92 years for Germany to pay its war debt!*

Adolf Hitler was the leader of the Nationalist Socialist Workers' Party – the Nazi Party. He was a speaker that grabbed people's attention, and told the German people he had the answers to their problems, promising to make Germany powerful and respected again. He blamed others for Germany's problems, especially the Jews. He also believed that the German race was better than all others –

something called Fascism – and we will see later that this led to some horrible events.

Hitler became the German Chancellor (the leader of the country) in 1933. He started to rebuild German's army, and invaded Rhineland and Austria, all of which was banned under the Treaty of Versailles, which aimed at stopping Germany going to war again.

One of Hitler's aims was to create something called 'Lebensraum' - living space. He wanted to expand Germany into Eastern Europe, to provide more land and resources for the German people, and this was one of the main causes of the war. In 1938, Germany invaded a region of Czechoslovakia (now the Czech Republic) called Sudetenland. He promised not to invade the rest of Czechoslovakia, but he broke that promise in March 1939. When he then invaded Poland in September 1939, World War 2 started.

It didn't end well for Hitler though. On April 29, 1945, with the war lost, he married Eva Braun in his Berlin bunker, and on April 30, he shot himself, while Eva Braun took poison. Their bodies were then burned.

AMAZING FACTS

Some facts about Hitler might surprise you!

- *Did you know that Hitler was not even German! He was born in 1889 in Austria.*

- *Hitler wanted to be an artist. He applied twice to join the Vienna Academy of Fine Arts, but was rejected both times.*
- *He was also rejected by the Austrian army for being unfit and too weak to fight.*
- *He fought in the German army in World War 1 and received the Iron Cross medal for bravery. He was wounded twice and could have died - in 1918, a British soldier, named Private Henry Tandey, spared Hitler's life, when he admitted he "couldn't shoot a wounded man". Without Hitler, maybe there would not have been a 2nd world war!*
- *He was Time Magazine man of the year in 1939!*
- *Hitler was called 'The Fuhrer' – German for leader. It was used by Hitler to emphasize his role as dictator with huge power.*
- *Hitler was tried for treason in 1923, after something called 'The Beer Hall Putsch' (Revolt), when he tried to overthrow the German government. He spent 1 year in prison.*
- *A law passed on September 15, 1935 stripped German Jews of their citizenship and forbid them from marrying people of 'German or related blood'.*
- *Berlin hosted the Olympics in 1936 – German Jews were not allowed to take part.*
- *There were several attempts to kill Hitler. One that came close was in July 1944, when a German Colonel called Claus von Stauffenberg planted a bomb that exploded during a meeting at Hitler's headquarters. It failed to kill Hitler!*

- *Hitler had an American nephew, called William Hitler. He served in the US Navy during the war and later changed his surname.*

After all that, it's time for our first hero!

Winston Churchill - Prime Minister of Britain

At the start of the war, the British Prime Minster was Neville Chamberlain. He tried to make a peace agreement with Hitler, but failed and so he was replaced as Prime Minister by Winston Churchill.

Churchill was the leader Britain needed – he was 65 years old in 1940, but had never ending energy, a cast-iron determination to win, and a great belief in Britain and its people.

Churchill could talk in a way that made people feel strong and brave. His words were like magic spells that could lift the spirits of a whole nation, particularly in the many dark times Britain faced.

In his first speech to Parliament as Prime Minister he said - *"I have nothing to offer but blood, toil, tears and sweat"* - and committed himself and the nation to all-out war until victory was achieved.

His speeches are still widely quoted today including:

"Never in the field of human conflict was so much owed by so many to so few." – this was in recognition of the sacrifice made by the RAF pilots in the Battle of Britain.

"*We shall fight on the beaches, we shall fight on the landing grounds, we shall fight in the fields and in the streets, we shall fight in the hills; we shall never surrender...*". Churchill's rallying cry to Britain to keep fighting, after the British Army's retreat from France at Dunkirk.

Churchill's defiance against Nazi Germany and his refusal to surrender or negotiate with Hitler during the early days of World War II, when Britain stood alone, made him a symbol of resistance and determination.

Winston Churchill

AMAZING FACTS

- *In photos from the time, you'll usually see him in a homburg hat, bow tie, with a large cigar and showing a V for Victory sign with his fingers.*
- *He joined the British Army in 1895 and fought in India, Sudan and South Africa.*
- *In his younger days, Churchill was a reporter in South Africa during the Boer War. He was captured and sent to prison. With no map or idea of the country, Churchill slipped past the guards, climbed the fence, and escaped. A large manhunt followed as he hid in coal mines and the bushes until he was smuggled out of South Africa and returned to Britain as a war hero.*
- *In 1953, Churchill won the Nobel Prize for Literature – he wrote over 50 books about history, World War 2 and biographies.*
- *He was a Member of Parliament for 64 years, spanning the reign of 6 monarchs - Victoria, Edward VII, George V, Edward VIII, George VI, and Elizabeth II.*
- *Despite winning the war, at the General Election of 1945, Churchill lost to the Labour Party led by Clement Atlee.*
- *In 2002, he was voted the 'Greatest Briton of All Time' in a BBC poll – he was actually half American (his mother was American).*

Our next person is a villain but he, and his country, fought with the Allies!

Josef Stalin – Leader of the Soviet Union

In war, sometimes you have to fight with people you don't like to beat the people you dislike even more and that's the case with Josef Stalin. Under Stalin, Russia joined the Allies to fight Hitler and the Nazis. But this was not before he made an agreement with Hitler's Germany to invade Poland and divide the country between Germany and Russia.

Josef Stalin

Russia's victory at the Battle of Stalingrad is seen as one of the major events that led to Germany's defeat. So we can definitely be thankful that he helped to defeat the Nazis.

But, and it's a big but! Stalin was definitely a villain!! He rose to prominence in the Russian Revolution, becoming General Secretary of the Communist Party in 1922, and seized power on Lenin's death in 1924. He was responsible for the death of at least 9 million people (and maybe up to 20 million)! He killed his political opponents, and millions of others were sent to Gulags, forced labour camps in the freezing conditions of Siberia where millions died, and others died from starvation between 1930-1933.

AMAZING FACTS

- *Stalin was not Russian – he was born in Georgia (part of the Russian Empire)*
- *His name at birth was Iosif Vissarionovich Djhugashvili but he changed it to Stalin in his 30s. He clearly thought he was a tough guy - Stalin means 'man of steel'!*
- *During WW II, Stalin ordered Red Army officers to execute deserters and troops who ran from battle. Between 1941 and 1942 alone, more than 150,000 soldiers were shot.*
- *Stalin was only 5 feet 4 inches tall. United States President Truman's nickname for Stalin was "the little squirt."*
- *Stalin often killed even his closest friends. He said, "I trust no one, not even myself."*
- *Russia trained over 2,000 women as snipers and many became the deadliest snipers in the whole Russian army, with some killing hundreds of Germans. One of these*

snipers was Lyudmila Pavlichenko, known to her enemies as "Lady Death,". She is the most successful female sniper in history with a total of 309 confirmed kills.

Let's turn to Italy, and their awful leader.

Benito Mussolini – Leader of Italy

Mussolini was a dictator who arrested political opponents, limited individual freedoms, and created a one-party state, and an environment of fear and control. He was the main founder of fascism (a belief in a master race and authoritarian rule or dictatorship) that would plunge Europe into war, and was a role model for Hitler.

In the 1930s, he tried to expand Italy's possessions, launching wars in Libya, Ethiopia, captured Albania and expanded Italian East Africa by capturing Somalia and Eritrea.

He formed a close alliance with Hitler, driving by his hunger for glory and empire, hoping to capture more territory during the war including Yugoslavia and Greece. But he was a terrible commander and made bad military choices, and the Italian army was not ready to fight, leading to Italy facing defeat in 1943. In 1945, Mussolini was captured, shot and hung upside down in public view.

AMAZING FACTS

- *It seems Mussolini was always violent! At age 10 he was expelled from school for stabbing a classmate in the hand, and stabbed another student at his next school.*

And now for the American President, one of the good guys!

Franklin D. Roosevelt, the 32nd President of the United States

President Roosevelt

Roosevelt guided the United States through much of the war, supporting the Allies before America officially entered the war following the attack on Pearl Harbor in December 1941. He worked closely with the Allied leaders, Winston Churchill of Britain and Joseph Stalin of the Soviet Union, to strategize and coordinate efforts against Nazi Germany and Imperial Japan.

Roosevelt was elected to a record four terms in office, serving from 1933 until his death in 1945, making him the longest-serving President in U.S. history. He died on April 12, 1945, just weeks before Germany's surrender, and was succeeded by his Vice President, Harry S. Truman.

AMAZING FACTS

- *Roosevelt was president for more than 12 years – the 22nd amendment now limits presidential terms to 8 years.*
- *He was paralysed from the waist down because of polio, but this was hidden from the public.*
- *He was the first president to travel by plane, and the first president to leave the country in wartime, when he took off from Miami in January 1943 aboard a Boeing 314 flying boat.*
- *He relocated by force 120,000 people of Japanese ancestry in America during the war. Americans were worried they might spy for Japan and so they were kept in camps.*

Allied Generals Front: Patton 2nd left, Eisenhower middle

And finally, the leader of Japan.

Hirohito, Emperor of Japan

Hirohito's reign spanned a tumultuous period in Japanese history, including the rise of militarism, Japan's involvement in World War II, and the subsequent post-war reconstruction. During his reign, Japan experienced significant political and social changes, including the country's transformation from a feudal society into a modern industrialized nation.

Hirohito's role during World War II remains controversial. While he was the symbolic head of state, the extent of his involvement in decision-making regarding Japan's military policies and wartime actions is not clear. After Japan's surrender in 1945, Hirohito kept his position as Emperor under the Allied occupation, but his powers were significantly reduced by the new Japanese constitution, which stripped him of his divine status and reduced him to a ceremonial role.

Throughout the post-war period, Hirohito played a crucial role in Japan's transition to democracy and its reconstruction efforts. He symbolized continuity and stability during a period of immense change, and he worked to promote peace and reconciliation both within Japan and with its former enemies.

Hirohito died on January 7, 1989, at the age of 87, after a reign of over 62 years.

AMAZING FACTS

- *When Hirohito announced the Japanese surrender on the radio in 1945, it was the first time the Japanese people had ever heard his voice.*

Other key figures in the war include General De Gaulle of France, Mao Tse-Tung of China, General MacArthur and General Patton of the USA, Field Marshall Montgomery of Britain, and the Nazis Jospeh Goebbels and Heinrich Himmler.

Enough of the leaders, let's look at some heroic soldiers who were actually involved in battle!

Audie Murphy

Murphy was the most decorated US soldier of WW2. He returned home a hero and became a famous actor. He won every medal available from the US army as well as French and Belgium awards for heroism.

In his most famous act, he jumped onto a burning tank and held back the enemy with a machine gun for almost an hour, killing 50 Germans.

Hershel Woodrow "Woody" Williams

Woody won the Medal of Honor for his unselfish act of bravery in Iwo Jima. At one point in the battle, he jumped onto a pillbox where Japanese soldiers were firing at the Americans and pushed his flamethrower into the vent killing the occupants. When he was later cornered, he single-handedly operated six flamethrowers against Japanese forces, keeping them at bay for several hours, all at the age of 21!

Desmond Doss

Doss was an unusual soldier – he refused to carry a gun as he didn't believe in killing people! He's remembered for saving 75 lives at Okinawa even though he was wounded 4 times! Over 12 hours, under enemy fire, he treated the wounded and lowered them to safety, down a cliff called Hacksaw

Ridge (now a famous film!). Even though he was wounded, he gave up his stretcher for another soldier.

Richard Bong

Bong was a hero of the skies! The greatest U.S. fighter ace of WW2, he destroyed 40 enemy planes during the war. He received 25 medals for his incredible feats plus the Medal of Honor.

In September 1944, even though his time in the air force was finished, he volunteered for more, and in 30 missions, he shot down 12 planes over Borneo and the Philippines. With over 200 missions and 500 hours of combat time, he was the top ace in the U.S. Air Force.

Charles Joseph Coward

A British soldier, Coward escaped seven times from German prisons during WW2, ultimately being sent to Auschwitz labor camp. One night, he smuggled himself in and out of the Auschwitz concentration camp where the Jews were held, and he reported back to the British what he'd seen. He became a witness during the trial of the Nazis at Nuremberg. Not only was he a master of escape himself, but he also helped 400 Jewish prisoners escape too!

Lachhiman Gurung

A Gurkha Rifleman, Gurung's unit was pinned down by the enemy as they threw hand grenades into their trench. Gurung threw two back but the third exploded in his hand.

Without his fingers on the right hand, he reloaded and fired with his left, keeping the enemy back by himself. At least 31 soldiers were killed by Gurung alone, in the four hours of the attack.

Jack Churchill

Known as "Fighting" Jack Churchill and "Mad Jack", this British trooper was known for his strange behavior. He fought with a longbow, arrows, and a Scottish broadsword! His used to say "any officer who goes into action without his sword is improperly armed". There's more! He used to charge into battle playing the bagpipes!

Even after a stint at the Sachsenhausen concentration camp (from which he escaped), he continued his military escapades, walking 93 miles to rejoin the army in Italy.

Not all heroes were soldiers. Below are some normal people, who took huge risks to help others.

Irena Sendler

Irena was a Polish social worker who took on the role of a nurse, so she could save over 2,500 Jewish babies and children by helping them escape and changing their identities once they were out of the Warsaw ghetto. By hiding them in ambulances, smuggling them through sewer pipes, or even carrying them out in suitcases, she saved many lives.

Raoul Wallenberg

Wallenberg was a Swedish businessman, but he was made a diplomat, so he could travel to Hungary, and assist in helping Jews escape. He managed to smuggle 100,000 Jews out of the country! He may have been arrested shortly before the end of the war and was either killed or died in prison.

Oskar Schindler

Made famous by the movie, Schindler's List, he was a German spy, and a Nazi party member, yet he ended up saving the lives of 1,200 Jews. He owned a factory, and ensured that all the Jews that he employed were kept safe through his contacts and financial contributions to Hitler's cause.

Chiune Sugihara

As a Japanese diplomat in Lithuania, he issued visas to Jews that he wrote by hand, saving over 6,000 lives. He even threw visas out of the train as he travelled, for Jews to collect and use to escape the country. He was given orders from Japan not to do so, but he did anyway and was removed from his job after the war ended.

Henryk Sławik

Sławik was a Polish politician who used his status and role to save 30,000 refugees. Almost a fifth of these were Jews to whom he had given false passports declaring they were

Catholics, so they could escape to freedom. His deeds were discovered, and he was executed.

Sir Nicholas Winton

In 1939, Winton rescued 669 mostly Jewish children, from Nazi-occupied Czechoslovakia. This was called the Czech kindertransport. Most children never saw their parents again; nearly all those left behind were murdered. He was so modest that he never told anyone what he had done. It wasn't until 50 years later that his wife found a scrapbook he'd kept and got in touch with 80 of the children he had rescued – one of whom is Lord Dubs who now sits in the British Parliament!

Sir Nicholas died in 2015 at the age of 106 years – a great age for an inspirational hero!

In later chapters, we're going to look at spies and code-breakers – more heroes who saved people and helped to shorten the length of the war.

4

THE BATTLE ZONES

Welcome to the chapter that will take you on a thrilling journey through the main battles of World War II, a time when the fate of nations hung in the balance. From the stormy beaches of Normandy to the vast deserts of North Africa, each battle is a piece of this grand puzzle, and together, they create a story of courage, sacrifice, and the triumph of good over evil. So, put on your imaginary helmets and gear up for a rollercoaster ride through the battles that shaped the course of history!

THE ROAD TO WAR

We start in Europe, on March 12, 1938 and the build up to the war. Hitler's army marched into neighbouring Austria and claimed the country as part of Nazi Germany. This was called the Anschluss. The Allies at the time did little to stop this – in fact, they went along with Hitler's demand for more land and agreed for Germany to takeover Sudetenland, a German-speaking region in Czechoslovakia, as long as he promised not to invade the rest of Czechoslovakia – in March 1939, he ignored this promise, and the world was on the way to war!

INVASION OF POLAND

After Austria and Czechoslovakia, Poland was next on Hitler's list of countries to invade to give Germany more land. He signed an agreement with Russia's Stalin agreeing that Germany would invade the west of Poland, and Russia would invade the east. Britain and France had promised to defend Poland if it was invaded – Hitler had not expected them to keep their promise.

On September 1, 1940, Germany invaded Poland and this was the real start of World War 2, with Britain and France keeping their promise, with both declaring war on Germany in support of Poland.

With over 9,000 artillery, 2,750 tanks, 2,000 aircraft, and 1.5 million soldiers, the Germans broke through Polish defences and quickly surrounded Warsaw, the capital city, where they began to inflict heavy bombing.

Poland was slow to mobilize its army, which had outdated guns and equipment compared with the modern German artillery. It also suffered the loss of many of their planes as the Luftwaffe had targeted them in the first days of the attack. The Polish army put up a brave defense, but with the Soviets entering from the east, they faced an impossible situation. The war was over in a few weeks. 66,000 Polish soldiers died, 133,000 were wounded, and 787,000 were taken captive.

Poland surrendered on September 28 and remained under Nazis occupation until close to the end of WW2.

Although Britain and France declared war as a result, neither of them was ready to engage in one. There was no Polish government left to free, so instead of rushing in, the war cooled down for six months before the next major offensive.

AMAZING FACTS

- *After Germany's invasion of Poland, the next six months of the war became known as the "Phony War" because there was almost no fighting in Europe. In Germany, this period was known as the Sitzkrieg ("Sitting War").*
- *The first official battle of WW2 was the Battle of WesterPlatte, fought near the Polish border with Germany.*

THE CONQUEST OF EUROPE

The next action happened in April 1940, when Germany invaded Denmark and Norway, after which Hitler turned his attention to the south.

The Nazis had a new way of fighting, and it caught the Allies off guard. The Allies were still planning for trench war, fighting as they had done in WWI. They were completely unprepared for the Germans' modern strategy of war - the Blitzkrieg, meaning Lightning War! Using tanks, artillery, and infantry together, the Nazis threw the Allies into chaos, punching through their defence, and beating them with speed. Germany gained a stunning victory, conquering Europe in just six weeks! (something that hadn't happened in the 5 years of WW1).

The Netherlands and Belgium were beaten in just a few days, before Germany marched on France and the Battle of France started. France thought it was safe from invasion, as it had built something called the Maginot Line – a 280 mile long line of concrete fortifications, with gun batteries, minefields and underground bunkers. It even had an underground railway! There was just one problem – it stopped at the Ardennes Forest. The French thought the Germans would attack in the same place they did in WW1, where the Maginot Line now was. They didn't think an army could get through the thick forest – but they were very wrong!

While the Germans sent a small force to attack the Maginot Line as a decoy, it sent 1 million men and 1,500 tanks through the Ardennes Forest. The Germans then raced through France before anyone knew what was going on! The British were forced to the coast and retreated across the Channel at Dunkirk. Paris was taken without a fight (the

French didn't want their beautiful capital to be bombed) and the French surrendered in June 1940.

German invasion route (Source: Wikimedia Commons)

AMAZING FACTS

- *To humiliate the French even more, Adolf Hitler ordered the French surrender document to be signed in the same* railway car where the Germans surrendered to France at the end World War I!

- The French army was one of the largest in the world but was beaten by a smaller army with better tactics.
- By the end of the Battle of France, the Allies had 360,000 casualties (dead and wounded) with 1.9 million prisoners taken, and 160,000 German and Italian casualties.
- At Dunkirk, 400,000 Allied soldiers were stranded, surrounded by Germans. A rescue effort called Operation Dynamo was launched, when 1,000 boats sailed from Britain – these included boats of all shapes and sizes, which became known as the 'Little ships of Dunkirk'. Among them was a paddle- steamer called the Medway Queen, which made 7 trips across The Channel, rescuing 7,000 men. The smallest boat to take part was the Tamzine, a fishing boat measuring just 15 feet (4.6 meters).
- Churchill expected only 45,000 soldiers to be rescued from Dunkirk – thanks to the effort of the small boats, 338,000 were rescued, enabling the British Amry to regroup and fight again.
- The British soldiers had to leave everything behind when evacuated from Dunkirk, including 46,000 vehicles and 400,000 tons of food.
- WW2 created the biggest refugee crisis in history. By 1940, 8 million Belgium, Dutch and French had to leave their homes, with nowhere to go.

BRITAIN UNDER ATTACK - THE BATTLE OF BRITAIN

Welcome to the first battle in history to be fought only in the air! By the summer of 1940, Britain stood alone against Nazi Germany. Hitler expected the British to discuss peace, but when this didn't happen, the war moved to the skies over Britain, as the Battle of Britain began a dazzling display of courage and resilience. This epic clash between the Royal Air Force (RAF) of Britain and the German Luftwaffe was a pivotal moment in World War II, a time when the fate of Britain hung in the balance.

77th Squadron Royal Air Force

Hitler was determined to conquer Britain. However, before he could launch a full-scale invasion, he needed to gain control of the skies.

The stage was set, and the players were ready. On one side, you had the daring pilots of the RAF, flying iconic planes like the Spitfire and Hurricane. These were the heroes of the story, young men with the weight of their country on their shoulders. On the other side were the German pilots, experienced and skilled pilots determined to clear the way for a German invasion.

The battle began in July 1940 and continued for several months. The British pilots were outnumbered but not outclassed, and fought the enemy in dogfights high above the English Channel. The skies became a canvas of swirling contrails and billowing clouds as planes danced in a deadly ballet.

The British radar system played a crucial role in the battle. The early warning system allowed the RAF to know where the Luftwaffe's was going to attack, giving the British pilots an important advantage. The radar operators became unsung heroes, providing vital information that often made the difference between victory and defeat.

Day after day, the pilots of both sides took to the skies, engaging in intense battles. The British, defending their homeland, fought with unmatched determination. The resilience of the RAF pilots became a symbol of hope for the British people, who watched as the drama unfolded above.

British Spitfire

The Luftwaffe, facing the British resistance, adjusted its tactics. Rather than targeting RAF airfields, they shifted their focus to bombing civilian centers, hoping to break the spirit of the British people. It was a dark chapter, known as the Blitz, where cities such as London faced relentless bombing. Yet, the British people remained unbroken.

As summer turned to autumn, the tide of the battle began to shift. The RAF, against all odds, emerged victorious. The German losses became too great, and Hitler postponed his invasion plans. The Battle of Britain was a triumph for the British, showing the country's courage, innovation, and determination.

Winston Churchill, the British Prime Minister, captured the spirit of the moment with his famous words: *"Never in the field of human conflict was so much owed by so many to so few."* The few were the brave pilots of the RAF, whose amazing spirit turned the tide of history.

AMAZING FACTS

- *Hitler's plan for the invasion of Britain was called Operation Sea Lion.*
- *By the end of August, the Luftwaffe has lost 600 planes compared to the RAF's 260.*
- *Many of the pilots in the Royal Air Force were from other countries such as Poland, Czechoslovakia, Canada, Australia, and South Africa. A Polish fighter squadron shot down the most German planes together during the war - 126.*
- *Sgt. Ray Holmes had no more ammunition when he saw a German bomber heading straight for Buckingham Palace, so he rammed into it with his wing, sending both aircraft crashing off course, and saving the palace.*
- *Fearing a German invasion, all road signs in Britain were removed, to confuse invading troops and possible German spies.*
- *Britain's valuable art was moved to secret locations. Paintings from the National Gallery were hidden in an underground mine in Wales. The Stone of Scone was moved from Westminster Abbey to a secret location, the details of which were sent to the Prime Minister of Canada to keep safe.*

- *Radar stands for 'radio detection and ranging'. The British radar system could detect enemy planes from 80 miles away, giving the British early warning of enemy attacks.*

BRITISH CITIES BOMBED - THE BLITZ

In the dark nights of World War II, a never-ending storm of destruction swept across the skies over Britain. This was the Blitz, a chapter of the war where the German Luftwaffe, like dark clouds of doom, unleashed a wave of bombing raids on British cities. It was a period of intense bombing that tested the strength and spirit of the British people.

Fireman tackling fires in the aftermath of a German raid.

Hitler had expected Britain to ask for peace talks and not to fight, but Churchill had other plans. The Blitz began in September 1940 and lasted for eight months. London was attacked the most, but cities across the country faced the onslaught. The German strategy was to break the will of the British people, to crush their spirit and force them into submission.

Imagine the night sky over London ablaze with the fiery glow of falling bombs. The air raid sirens wailing, signaling families to seek shelter in underground bunkers. The hum of German planes and the droning of their engines became a haunting soundtrack to the nightly ordeal. On the first night, 350 German bombers dropped their bombs over London, killing 450 people and injuring 1,500. This bombing of London continued every night for 57 nights.

The city's iconic landmarks, like St. Paul's Cathedral and the Houses of Parliament, stood defiant against the onslaught. Amid the chaos, ordinary citizens became heroes. Firefighters battled the infernos, rescue workers pulled survivors from the rubble, and the Home Guard patrolled the streets, determined to defend their neighborhoods.

Children were evacuated from the cities to the countryside, seeking safety from the raining bombs. Families huddled in makeshift shelters, enduring the terror from below as the ground shook and the thunderous explosions echoed through the night. Over 100,000 people sheltered in the

London Underground every night, sleeping on the platforms.

But amidst the devastation, a remarkable spirit emerged. The British people refused to be broken. They found comfort in communal shelters, shared stories of resilience, and displayed a remarkable sense of humor in the face of adversity. The phrase "*Keep Calm and Carry On*" became a rallying cry, reminding the people to remain strong in the face of danger.

London's East End, a working-class area that bore the brunt of the attacks, became a symbol of resilience. The Cockney spirit prevailed, with locals displaying a remarkable ability to find humor even in the darkest moments. They danced in the rubble, sang defiant songs, and stood tall against the storm of destruction.

Even after 8 months of bombing, with 43,000 civilians killed and with 1 million homes destroyed, the British people stayed strong, and it became one of the most important things we remember about how amazing they were during the war. The Germans couldn't break the British and gave up the bombing campaign.

AMAZING FACTS

- *The city of Coventry had so many explosives dropped on it on November 14, 1940, that the smell of burning buildings reached up to the pilots of the German bombers flying overhead. 50% of the city was destroyed in just one night!*

- *A 1-ton bomb landed near St Paul's Cathedral, an iconic landmark in London that Churchill said should be saved at all cost. The bomb didn't explode and soldiers spent 3 days digging the bomb out of its crater. It was diffused and then driven to the countryside to be detonated by Robert Davies – it was thought to be a suicide mission as bumps in the road could have detonated the bomb at any moment. For his effort, Davies was given the George Cross and St Paul's was saved!*
- *In Operation Columba, the British parachuted over 16,000 homing pigeons into occupied Europe, each carrying some paper and a pencil to try and gain intelligence on the enemy. The Germans responded by punishing people with the death penalty if they didn't hand the pigeons in. They also trained hawks to kill the pigeons. The pigeons were considered so important that MI5 (the British Intelligence Service) set up the Falcon Destruction Unit to kill any enemy birds attacking their pigeons. Only one in ten returned alive, but some provided crucial information.*
- *Unexploded bombs are still found in Britain. In February 2024, a 1,000lbs (500kg) bomb was found in a garden in Plymouth, England. 10,000 people were evacuated from their homes while bomb disposal experts dug up the bomb, transported it the sea and detonated under the water!*
- *1 in 10 bombs on Britain and Germany didn't explode.*
- *From 1940, churches in Britain were forbidden to ring their bells. They were only to be rung to signal a German invasion.*

THE SIEGE OF LENINGRAD

By 1941, Hitler had conquered as far west in Europe as he could, and after giving up his plan to invade Britain, he turned to the east. Operation Barbarossa was the German plan to invade the Soviet Union. The German army was smaller and less powerful than the Soviets, but Hitler thought that force and speed would be enough to win him victory. The Germans assembled 3 million men, 7,000 artillery pieces and 2,500 aircraft for the invasion, the biggest in history.

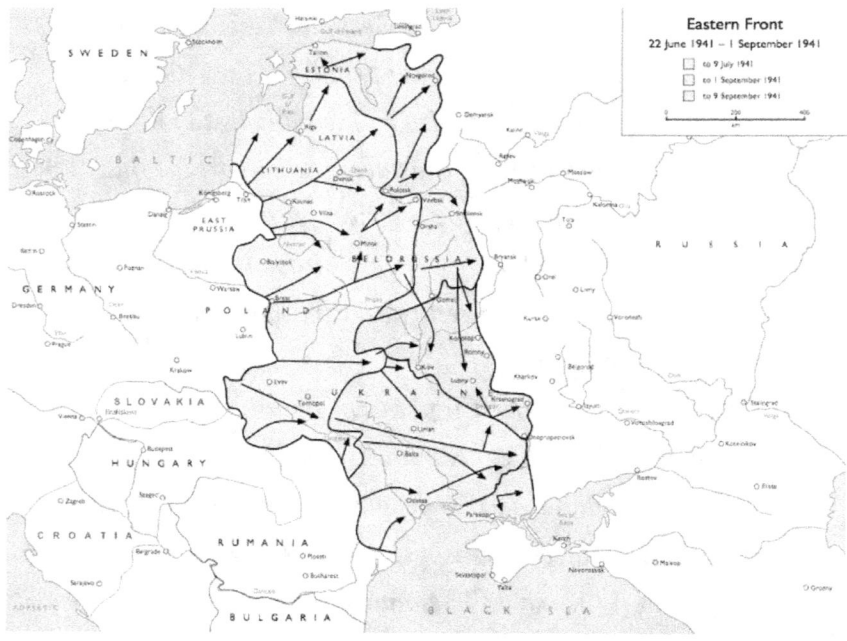

*Map of the Eastern Front 1941 showing German invasion of Soviet Union
(Source: Wikimedia Commons)*

The cold Russian winter made fighting difficult, tanks got stuck in the snow and there was a lack of food and ammunition. The Germans were within 200 miles of Moscow when they stopped. The other major target of the German invasion was the city of Leningrad. Rather than trying to capture the city, Hitler decided to lay siege to it instead.

In the heart of the Soviet Union, a city stood bravely against the relentless onslaught of war. This was Leningrad (now called St. Petersburg), a city that would suffer one of the most distressing and longest sieges in history. The Siege of Leningrad became a testament to the strength and endurance of the human spirit in the face of unimaginable suffering.

As the German Army advanced deep into Soviet territory in 1941, 500,000 Germans marched on Leningrad and surrounded it. Hitler's plan was to cut off the city from the rest of the world, trapping its residents and starving them into submission. The siege began in September 1941, and what followed would be 872 days (that's almost 2 years!) of unbelievable hardship, deprivation, and a huge will to survive. Hitler also wanted to destroy the city and the Luftwaffe dropped over 75,000 bombs on it.

The siege cut off all supply routes, leaving the city isolated and vulnerable. Food, fuel, and essential supplies became scarce. The harsh Russian winter added another layer of misery, as temperatures plummeted, and the city was blanketed in snow.

The blockade cut off the city from the rest of the country, but it did not break the spirit of the people. Despite facing starvation, the residents created gardens on rooftops and in any available open space, cultivating vegetables in the frozen soil. Every resource was conserved, and the city's residents shared what little they had with one another.

As the siege dragged on, the city's inhabitants faced a severe lack of food. Rations were tiny, and people were constantly hungry. It was this lack of food that killed most people. People were allowed just 3 slices of bread a day!

But, in the face of starvation, the people of Leningrad displayed an extraordinary will to live. They ate whatever they could find, from rats and pets to wallpaper and even leather, and their stories of survival show how incredibly strong people can be. Some people turned to cannibalism, eating other people!

The only supplies trickled in through a gap along Lake Ladoga, but even this was not nearly enough. Furniture and books were burned to keep warm as temperatures dropped.

It was not until January 1944 that the siege was finally lifted, as the Soviet forces managed to break through the German lines. The city, scarred but undefeated, emerged from the darkness.

Of the 3 million people that were stuck in Leningrad from the beginning of the siege, an estimated 1.5 million people died or were killed, but it had not broken the spirit of the city or its people.

AMAZING FACTS

- *There were more Russian deaths during the Siege of Leningrad than the United States and Britain combined had in all of WW2.*
- *The Germans used over 600,000 horses in its invasion of the Soviet Union.*
- *Four of every five German soldiers killed in the war died in its battle with Russia.*

THE UNITED STATES ENTERS THE WAR - PEARL HARBOR

For many years before WW2, Japan had become more aggressive to its neighbours and had wanted to restore its past glory by expanding its territory. As part of this, Japan invaded China in 1931, reaching Beijing in 1937. Japan is an island with limited natural resources, so it wanted to take resources from China instead. Japan was also bitter from being left empty handed from the Treaty of Versailles at the end of WW1.

On December 7, 1941, the people of Pearl Harbor in Hawaii (a chain of Islands in the Pacific and a state of America) woke up to a sunny day. Little did they know that danger was lurking in the sky. Suddenly, like fierce dragons appearing from the clouds, Japanese planes swooped down in a surprise attack.

Carrier capsizing

The attack on Pearl Harbor was quick and intense. The Japanese planes targeted the American naval base, destroying battleships, airplanes, and more. The sound of explosions and the sight of smoke filled the air. It was like a storm of chaos had descended upon this once tranquil harbor.

The reason behind this sudden attack was that Japan wanted to expand its power in the Pacific, and the only thing standing in its way was the American navy. So, it launched a surprise attack, thinking it would weaken America's ability to fight back. The Americans thought any attack would come from the sea not the air. There had been several warning signs, but they were ignored. 200 Japanese planes attacked the US airfields, destroying 300 US planes.

The consequences of the attack were enormous. Many soldiers lost their lives, and numerous ships were damaged or sunk. The most significant loss was the USS Arizona battleship, killing over 1,000 men. It remains underwater at Pearl Harbor as a memorial, a symbol of the lives sacrificed on that fateful day.

In less than 2 hours, 2,500 people had been killed and every American ship damaged. Despite this damage, many important American ships were at sea, and survived to attack Japan later.

The attack on Pearl Harbor shocked not only the people of Hawaii but the entire world. It was a wake-up call, shaking nations into realizing that they were now truly in a world at war. The United States, which had tried to stay out of the conflict, could no longer stand on the sidelines.

In the days following the attack, the United States declared war on Japan, officially entering World War II. This event united the American people like never before. Young men volunteered to join the military, and the entire nation rallied together to support the war effort. The attack on Pearl Harbor was a turning point in the war, bringing the full force of the United States into the war, not just against Japan, but also against Germany and the war in Europe.

Pearl Harbor

AMAZING FACTS

- The Japanese ships all kept radio silence up until the attack when the words "Tora! Tora! Tora!" (Tiger! Tiger! Tiger!) were broadcast as a code that meant the invasion was successful.
- Japanese kamikaze pilots would deliberately crash their planes into enemy targets. Around 3,600 died in these suicide missions.
- Within 30 days of the attack, 134,000 Americans had signed up to be part of the military. Fifty million would eventually be employed as part of the war effort.

- *One of the most highly decorated U.S. Army units that fought in Europe in 1944 were the 442nd Regimental Combat Team that was made up entirely of 14,000 Japanese Americans.*
- *After entering the war, all car manufacturers in America instead focused on making military vehicles. While 3 million cars were made in 1941, just 139 were made from 1942 to 1945!*
- *To avoid food sounding German, America tried to rename the hamburger (named after the German town of Hamburg) as the 'liberty steak' – it didn't catch on! What did catch on was the renaming of the frankfurter (named after the German city of Frankfurt) to 'hot dog'!*

SKIES ABLAZE IN THE PACIFIC – THE BATTLE OF MIDWAY

After the Japanese bombing of Pearl Harbour, the USA declared war on Japan, and Germany then declared war on America, bringing America properly into World War 2. What happened next? Well, there were no immediate battles although in April 1942, 16 American B25s bombed targets in Tokyo. There wasn't much damage, but it shocked the Japanese that their mainland could be bombed and afterwards, kept 600 fighter jets in Japan for defence, planes that otherwise could be used in other battles, so it was a good outcome for the Americans.

It took 5 months before the first major battle against Japan - but in that time, the US called up men to fight and built new factories to make weapons.

Both sides were looking to control the Pacific and its islands – this would give the Japanese bases closer to America from which they could launch attacks, and the Americans wanted to drive the Japanese out of all the islands and countries it had invaded in Asia, such as Burma, Singapore and Malay (now Malaysia), drive them back to Japan and beat them.

In May 1942, the battles started, kicking off with the Battle of the Coral Sea, fought off New Guinea, near Australia. The Americans were able to break Japan's secret war code and knew the Japanese plans. The battle that followed was the first air-naval battle in history, and in all, 70 Japanese and 66 American planes were destroyed. The battle lastest 4 days with no real winner.

Let's turn to the Battle of Midway. The Japanese saw the control of Midway as hugely important, being roughly halfway between Japan and America, which would allow it to control the Pacific and attack America – even though it is still 3,200 miles from San Francisco!

Fought over 3 days from June 4, the naval Battle of Midway saw the Americans beat the Japanese, altering the course of the war, allowing it to start its 'island hopping' campaign across the Pacific and forcing the Japanese to retreat.

The victory at Midway was mainly due to codebreakers. Cryptanalysts had been hard at work trying to decipher the Japanese messages and had identified that the Japanese were targeting a place known only as "AF." The American base at Midway sent out false communication that there was no fresh water there, and soon after a Japanese message came through confirming "AF" had water problems. They knew where Japan would attack, and when, so the Americans setup an ambush!

Japan's initial attack was successful as they damaged the base at Midway, but what they were not expecting was an extra U.S. Naval force that had been hidden until that point. Aircraft from the U.S. carriers launched attacks on the Japanese sinking 3, called Akagi, Kaga, and Soryu.

The last of the main ships, the Hiryu, managed to send planes that hit the USS Yorktown. But by the afternoon, the Americans had another wave of aircraft that put the Hiryu out of action. Fighting continued for two days, but with Japan's carriers damaged, they were finally forced to retreat.

The Japanese lost over 3,000 men, four aircraft carriers, and more than 300 planes compared to the United States' 362 men, one carrier, a destroyer, and 140 aircraft.

AMAZING FACTS

- The Battle of the Coral Sea was the first naval battle in history where the 2 opposing navies never saw each other or fired directly at each other!

- In February 1942, the American mainland was attacked in Oregon, when a Japanese submarine fired 16 shells at Ellwood Oil Field, but the damage was minimal. However, it did spark panic among the public.
- Oregon was also bombed by a Japanese aircraft, where a floatplane dropped incendiary bombs, hoping to start a forest fire, but this attack failed.
- Japan also launched balloon bombs against America. They were launched 5,000 miles from the US, crossing the Pacific Ocean at 30,000 feet. Their bombs were designed to be dropped after 3 days – 350 bombs made it to America, to 15 states including Michigan and Iowa, and were shot down by the US military.

THE BATTLE OF STALINGRAD - HISTORY'S BLOODIEST BATTLE?

A legendary battle was fought during the cold winter of 1942-1943. This was no ordinary battle; it was the Battle of Stalingrad, a clash between the mighty armies of Nazi Germany and the resilient forces of the Soviet Union. This epic showdown would become one of the turning points of World War II.

The city of Stalingrad (now called Volgograd, in southwest Russia), located on the banks of the Volga River, became the battleground where the fate of Russia would be decided. The

German forces, under the command of General Friedrich Paulus, aimed to capture Stalingrad and gain control of the vital Volga River, a lifeline for the Soviet Union. Little did they know that the Soviets, led by General Vasily Chuikov, were prepared to defend their city with unwavering determination.

As the icy winds swept through the ruins of Stalingrad, the two armies clashed in a brutal struggle for dominance. The urban landscape became a maze of destroyed buildings, rubble-strewn streets, and hidden dangers as almost every building was knocked down by explosions. It was a battleground like no other, where soldiers fought not only against each other but also against the harsh winter conditions.

The German forces, equipped with tanks, artillery, and a powerful war machine, initially made significant advances. They captured key areas of the city, inching closer to their goal. However, the Soviets, refusing to retreat, fought fiercely – anyone who deserted their post was shot! The ruined buildings became strongholds, the Germans struggled to move around or find the Soviet soldiers and every street corner turned into a battlefield.

The Battle of Stalingrad was not only fought by soldiers; it was a struggle for survival for the civilians caught in the crossfire. The city's residents faced unimaginable hardships as they sought shelter in basements and cellars, enduring hunger, cold, and constant fear. The city itself, reduced to a skeleton of its former self, bore witness to the relentless carnage.

As the winter set in, the conditions worsened. The German soldiers faced the bitter cold without adequate supplies, while the Soviets, despite being surrounded, held on with bravery. The Soviets, in a daring move, launched a counteroffensive, encircling the German forces in what would become one of the largest and deadliest encirclements in history.

The turning point had come. The trapped German forces, facing starvation and frostbite, struggled to hold their ground. Despite desperate attempts to break the encirclement, they were surrounded, and surrender became inevitable (even though Hitler had forbidden the Germans to surrender – he expected them to fight to the last man!).

In February 1943, after 200 days of brutal fighting and suffering, the German Sixth Army, once a formidable force, surrendered to the Soviets. The battle is often considered one of the deadliest in history – up to 2 million people were killed, including soldiers and civilians. The Battle of Stalingrad had ended, and the Soviet Union had won, marking a significant shift in momentum on the Eastern Front.

AMAZING FACTS

- *The first defenders of Stalingrad were women from the 1077th Anti-Aircraft Regiment. Most were teenage girls, just out of school, who held off the German advance for*

two days. When their position was finally overrun by the overwhelming German assault, the Germans were surprised to find they had been fighting girls!
- *The battle was the largest of the 2nd World War and maybe in all history, with 2.2 million people taking part.*
- *Food was in short supply, so people ate rats and mice and in some cases each other!*
- *A Russian sniper called Vasily Zaitsev, killed at least 265 enemy soldiers in the battle.*
- *Of the 3 million Germans taken prisoner by Russia, 1 million died in captivity. Of the 91,000 who surrendered at Stalingrad, just 6,000 made it back to Germany!*

BATTLE IN NORTH AFRICA'S DESERT – EL ALAMEIN

In the vast and sun-scorched deserts of North Africa, a pivotal chapter of World War II unfolded - the Battle of El Alamein. This epic clash marked a turning point in the war in the deserts, giving the winning side control of Egypt and the Suez Canal.

Imagine a vast sea of golden sands, stretching as far as the eye can see, dotted with tanks, soldiers, and the rumble of war machines. El Alamein, a small railway stop in the Egyptian desert, became the stage for a dramatic confrontation that would determine the fate of North Africa.

The battle began on October 23, 1942, when the British Eighth Army, under the leadership of General Bernard

Montgomery, launched a massive attack against the Axis forces commanded by General Erwin Rommel, known as the "Desert Fox." The Allies were determined to stop the Axis advance and push them out of North Africa.

British Commander, Field Marshal Montgomery

The battle unfolded in two main phases – the First Battle of El Alamein and the Second Battle of El Alamein. The First Battle saw initial successes for the Axis forces, but as the battle lines shifted, the Allies held their ground. Both sides were locked in tough tank battles, with the desert becoming a maze of armored vehicles moving through the sands.

It was during the Second Battle of El Alamein, which started on October 23, 1942, that the tide turned in favor of the Allies. General Montgomery, known for his detailed planning and strategic brilliance, led a carefully coordinated attack. With double the number of tanks and soldiers as the Germans, the battle lines echoed with the thunder of artillery and the roar of tanks as the Allies launched a massive assault.

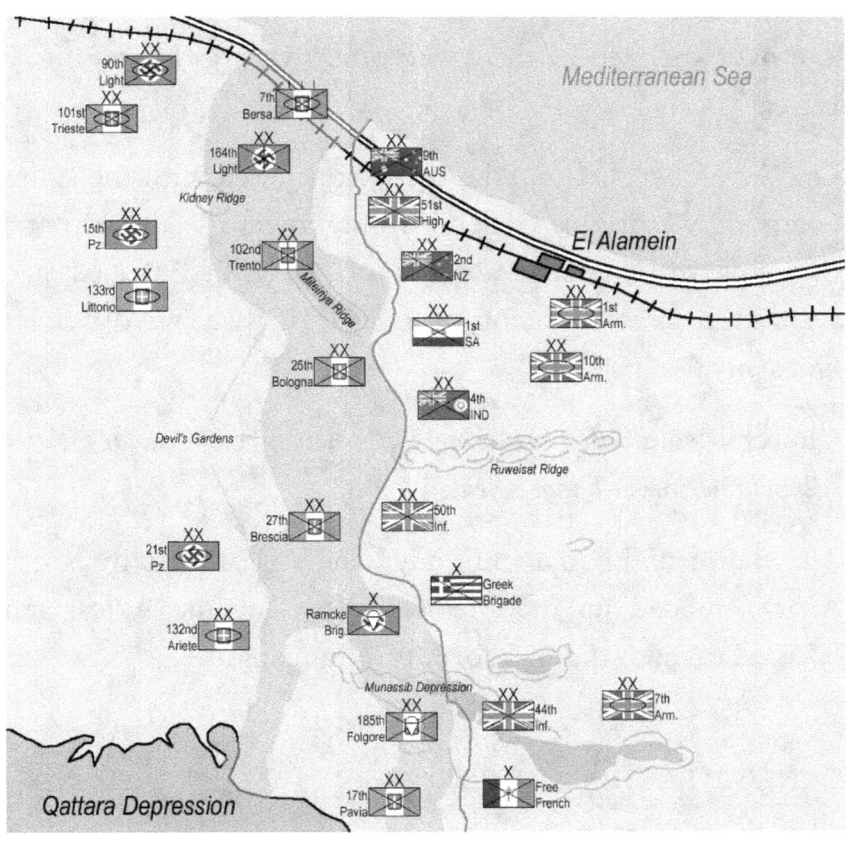

2nd Battle of El Alamein - deployment of forces on the eve of battle (Source Wikimedia Commons)

The turning point came with Operation Lightfoot, a massive infantry and artillery assault that punched a hole through the Axis defenses. The Allies, including British, Australian, New Zealand, South African, Indian, and Free French troops, pushed forward with relentless determination.

Imagine the night sky over El Alamein lit up by flares and explosions as the Allies relentlessly advanced. The battle raged for days, and Rommel, facing a shortage of supplies and overwhelmed by the Allied offensive, was forced into a retreat.

On November 4, 1942, the battle concluded with the Allies emerging victorious. General Montgomery's leadership and the unwavering determination of the Allied troops had secured a crucial victory the first British victory over Germany.

Churchill said: *"Before Alamein, we never had a victory. After Alamein, we never had a defeat."*

The Battle of El Alamein ended the Axis threat in North Africa, opened up the Mediterranean for the Allies, and boosted their confidence for future campaigns.

TANKS CLASH AT KURSK

Most historians point to D-Day being the moment when the tide turned against the Germans, but the Battle of Kursk was a crushing defeat from which the Germans never recovered.

It was Hitler's last attempt to gain an advantage in Russia and he failed.

Imagine a landscape of endless fields, stretching as far as the eye can see. Kursk, a key location in western Russia, became the battleground where the Soviet Union would face the German forces in a showdown of huge proportions. The stage was set for a clash that would test the strength and strategies of both sides.

The Germans, still reeling from their defeat at Stalingrad, wanted to regain momentum on the Eastern Front. On the other side, the Soviets, buoyed by their success in halting the German advance, were determined to defend their homeland and push the invaders back. The result was a massive collision of armies – 780,000 German troops and 1.9 million Soviets - and the largest tank battle in history, involving 6,000 tanks, 2 million troops, and 4,000 aircraft.

The Battle of Kursk, starting on July 5, 1943, involved intense planning and preparation on both sides. The Germans, under the command of Field Marshal Erich von Manstein, aimed to encircle and destroy a bulge in the Soviet lines near Kursk. Meanwhile, the Soviets, led by Generals Georgy Zhukov and Konstantin Rokossovsky, were ready to face the German onslaught.

The battlefield became a maze of trenches, minefields, and defensive fortifications. The Soviets, learning from previous battles, had created a formidable defensive line known as the Kursk Salient. This defensive belt was designed to absorb and blunt the force of the German attack, setting the stage for a counteroffensive.

The Battle of Kursk unfolded in two main phases - the German offensive known as Operation Citadel and the Soviet counteroffensive. The Germans initiated the battle with a massive assault on the Kursk Salient, using a vast number of tanks, artillery, and infantry. However, the Soviets, anticipating the attack, had fortified their positions and were ready to resist.

The German advance encountered fierce resistance as Soviet tanks and infantry fought valiantly to defend their positions. The battlefield became a storm of fire and steel, with tanks engaging in intense duels and infantry engaged in close-quarters combat. The Soviets, utilizing a strategy of defense in depth, absorbed the German assault and slowly began to turn the tide.

The Soviet counteroffensive, known as Operation Kutuzov, was launched in response to the weakened German forces. The Red Army, with fresh reserves and a well-coordinated plan, pushed the Germans back, creating a series of encirclements. The Battle of Prokhorovka, a major tank battle within Kursk, became one of the largest tank battles in history, with thousands of tanks clashing in a brutal showdown.

By August 23, 1943, the Battle of Kursk had concluded with a decisive Soviet victory. The Germans, unable to break the fortified Soviet lines and facing substantial losses, were forced into a retreat. The Battle of Kursk marked a significant turning point in the Eastern Front, shifting the momentum in favor of the Soviets, who went on the offensive, reclaiming territories previously occupied by the Germans.

There were massive casualties on both sides, with estimates ranging from hundreds of thousands to over a million killed, wounded, or missing. The battle inflicted heavy losses on the German Army, weakening its ability to conduct further offensives in the East.

AMAZING FACTS

- *Soviet Commander Nikolai Vatutin ordered his tanks to be buried, so the Germans could only see the top, and be drawn in closer. This eliminated the advantage of the German long-range guns, and protected the Soviet tanks.*
- *While the Soviets lost far more men (800,000) and equipment, the German losses were unsustainable. Germany suffered 200,000 casualties from a force of 780,000 men.*
- *Two days prior to the Battle of Prokhorovka, Allied forces had landed on Sicily commencing their Italian Campaign. The invasion forced Hitler to cancel Operation Citadel on July 12 and divert his forces from the Eastern Front to Italy.*

ALLIED INVASION OF EUROPE - D-DAY

By 1944, the Allies had been planning a major invasion of German-occupied Western Europe for several years. The invasion was crucial for opening up a second front against Nazi Germany, which would alleviate pressure on the Soviet Union in the east and potentially lead to the downfall of Adolf Hitler's regime.

D-Day, which stands for "Day of Decision" or "Designated Day," refers to June 6, 1944, when Allied forces launched the largest amphibious invasion in history during World War II. The operation was a pivotal moment in the war, marking the beginning of the end for Nazi Germany's control over Europe.

Without any harbors or ports on mainland Europe under Allied control, troops would need to land at Normandy, the only accessible beach head. But the Germans were ready for them, and it would need to be one of the biggest combined naval, air, and land operations ever to make it a success.

June 6–August 30

Eisenhower had started working on plans for different scenarios for an invasion, codenamed "Operation Overlord" as early as 1941. Once the politicians had agreed, troops from 12 different countries had begun assembling months before, preparing for the invasion of Nazi-occupied France. These consisted mainly of soldiers from America, Britain, and Canada, but there were divisions that joined from

Australia, Belgium, Czechoslovakia, Holland, France, Greece, New Zealand, Norway, Rhodesia, South Africa, and Poland.

AMAZING FACTS

- *To build up resources for the invasion, British factories increased production, and in the first half of 1944, 9 million tons of supplies and equipment crossed from North America to Britain. Over 1.4 million American servicemen arrived during 1943–1944 to take part in the invasion.*
- *To support the invasion, huge pipelines were laid across the sea from Britain to France to carry fuel for the invasion, something never done before.*

Hitler was aware of the impending invasion, although he was not sure where it would take place. Rommel was given the task of fortifying the coastline, and ended up constructing 2,400 miles of bunkers, minefields with 4 million mines, and other obstacles that came to be known as the "Atlantic Wall".

To throw the enemy off, the Allies launched "Operation Bodyguard" to fool the Germans into thinking they would invade at Calais, the shortest distance across the English Channel from England. False radio transmissions and radar pictures were broadcast of inflatable tanks and dummy landing craft in Kent. These proved successful enough to delay Hitler and Rommel from moving their army to Normandy for seven weeks.

The five main beaches targeted during the Normandy landings on D-Day were given code names by the Allies. These code names were used for planning and coordination purposes:

- Utah Beach - Located on the westernmost flank of the invasion area. It was assigned to American forces, specifically the U.S. 4th Infantry Division.
- Omaha Beach - Situated to the east of Utah Beach, Omaha Beach was another American landing site. It was one of the most heavily fortified and defended beaches, and the assault there resulted in significant casualties among American troops.
- Gold Beach - Positioned between Omaha Beach to the west and Juno Beach to the east, Gold Beach was assigned to British forces, primarily the British 50th Infantry Division.
- Juno Beach - Situated between Gold Beach to the west and Sword Beach to the east, Juno Beach was assigned to Canadian forces, specifically the Canadian 3rd Infantry Division.
- Sword Beach - The easternmost landing site, Sword Beach was designated for British forces, particularly units from the British 3rd Infantry Division and the 1st Special Service Brigade.

These code names helped facilitate communication and planning among the Allied forces during the D-Day invasion of Normandy on June 6, 1944.

On June 6, paratroopers were sent in ahead to secure key bridges that would be needed once the soldiers landed on the beaches. By the time the landing crafts began to hit the beach and unload their men, the airborne division had successfully captured the bridges.

Allied aircraft drop paratroopers in advance of D-Day

At 6:30 a.m. British and Canadian troops stormed onto Gold, Juno, Utah, and Sword beaches with little resistance. However, the fifth beach of Omaha was more of a battle. The Germans had stationed their machine gunners at Omaha, but after suffering more than 2,000 casualties, the Americans finally pushed inland.

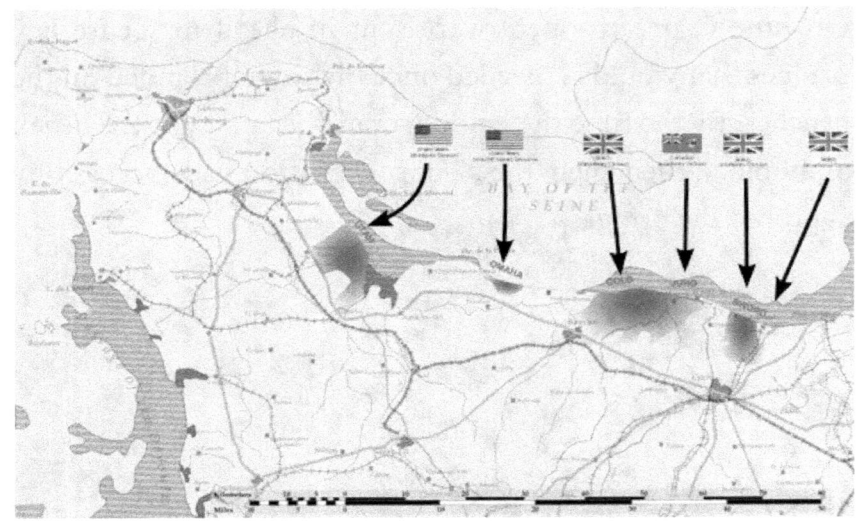
Map of the D-Day Landing Beaches (Source: Wikimedia Commons)

On that first day, 156,000 infantrymen stormed the beaches, three times the number of Germans that were stationed there to hold them off. Without Rommel to oversee events, the German response was delayed, but after some time, Hitler ordered Panzer units to drive through to Sword and Juno beaches that would have completely crippled the landings. But they were met with stiff resistance from anti-tank gunners who held them off.

Beach Landing

Over the next few days, a total of 2.5 million men were ferried onto the beaches along with 500,000 vehicles and a mass of supplies. Although the Germans were putting up fierce resistance, they were running out of reinforcements, and had very few Luftwaffe to assist in the air. On top of that, they were running out of officers, some of whom died, while others were dismissed for admitting defeat.

Omaha Beach after D-Day. Protected by barrage balloons, ships delivered trucks loaded with supplies.

AMAZING FACTS

- *There were no harbors that could be used on the Normandy coast, so two ready-built harbors were taken in sections across the English Channel and assembled off Omaha Beach and Gold Beach. The Mulberry harbors were to be used until major French ports could be captured and brought back into use after repair. Parts of these harbors can still be seen off the Normandy beaches today.*
- *When landing on the beaches, Allied troops had to dodge the German bullets, the 100 million mines that had been laid, the barbed wire and anti-tank girders.*

At the end of June, the Port of Cherbourg was taken back from the Germans, a tactical victory that opened the way for more ships and supplies to be brought in. Up until that time, ready-built harbors had been designed with floating piers, but the weather caused these to be less effective than beach landings using different vessels.

Germans Changing Signposts

July 25 saw the Americans break through a gap in the German's tank line, and despite Hitler's attempts to squash it, they advanced. By that stage, the Nazi strongholds were being overrun, and the order was given for the Germans to withdraw. Even though the bridges had been destroyed, they still managed to cross the Seine to safety with the Allies moving up behind them.

As the enemy raced across the border, French resistance forces revolted against the Germans in Paris. Eisenhower changed direction, and instead of bypassing Paris, he reinforced the fighting on August 24. The following morning, the Nazi commander of the city surrendered. Operation Overlord had reached all its objectives, but with 300,000 German soldiers, and 200,000 Allied soldiers perishing as a result.

D-Day remains one of the most significant military operations in history, symbolizing the courage, sacrifice, and cooperation of Allied forces in the fight against tyranny. It was a pivotal moment in World War II, shaping the course of history and ultimately leading to the downfall of Nazi Germany.

AMAZING FACTS

- *A practice run for D-Day was staged two months before along an English beach. It was called "Exercise Tiger," and the Germans found out about it, and torpedoed American landing ships killing 749 soldiers.*
- *On July 20, 1944, Claus von Stauffenberg attempted to assassinate Hitler, inside his Wolf's Lair field headquarters. Hitler survived when a bomb planted in a briefcase exploded but failed to kill him after one of his generals moved the case to get a better look at a map.*

ISLAND HOPPING IN THE PACIFIC – THE BATTLE OF IWO JIMA

Japan had invaded Korea in 1910 and Manchuria in 1931. In 1937, it invaded China and in 1942 in overran many European colonies in South-East Asia, including Burma, French Indochina and Singapore. US forces and other Allied troops 'island hopped' their way through South-East Asia, forcing the Japanese to retreat towards Japan.

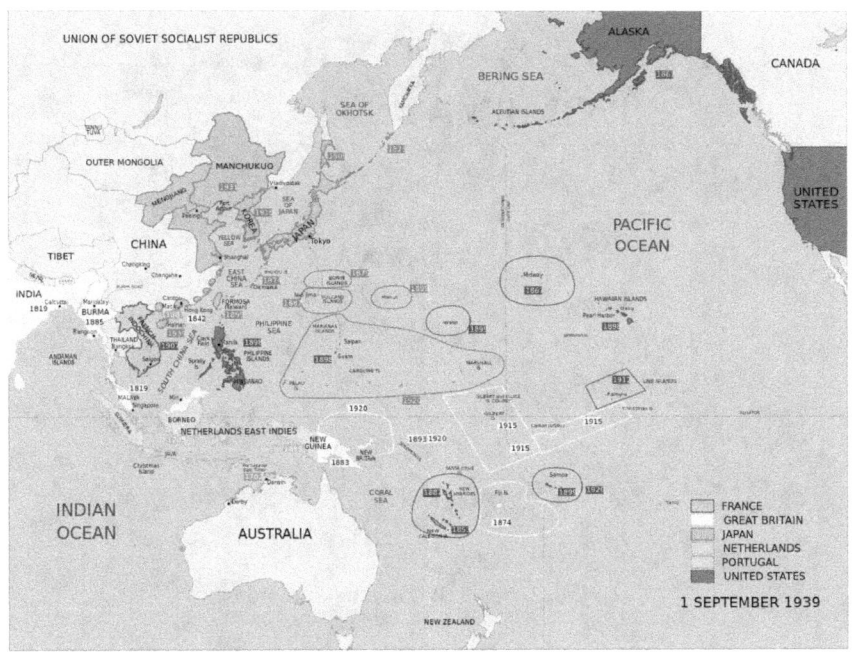

Asia-Pacific Region 1939 (Source: Wikimedia Commons)

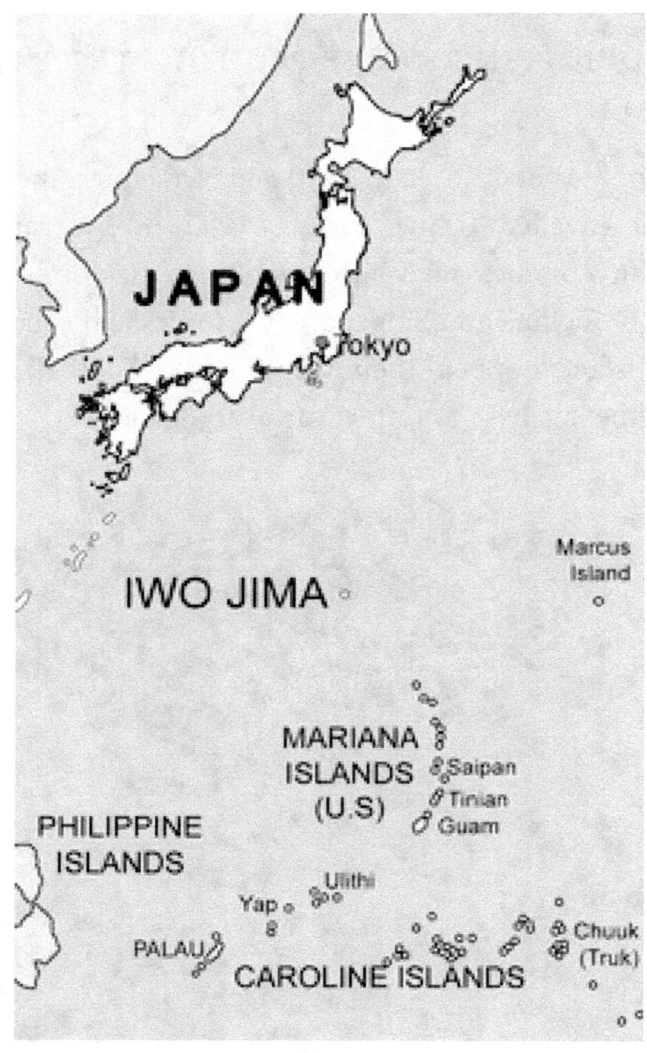

Iwo Jima (Source: Wikimedia Commons)

Iwo Jima is a small volcanic island located in the Pacific Ocean, 750 miles from Tokyo. Its strategic importance lay in its potential use as an airbase by American bombers targeting the Japan. Capturing Iwo Jima would provide a crucial staging area for further Allied offensives against Japan.

The battle was meticulously planned by Allied commanders, who recognized the formidable challenges posed by the island's terrain and Japanese defenses. The Japanese had heavily fortified the island with an intricate network of underground tunnels, bunkers, and concealed artillery positions.

Iwo Jima Fighting

The Americans bombed the island for 9 months, before launching the ground assault with 30,000 soldiers. On February 19, 1945, the United States Marine Corps launched a massive amphibious assault on Iwo Jima. The initial landing was met with intense resistance from Japanese defenders entrenched on the island. The Marines faced heavy machine gun fire, artillery barrages, and kamikaze attacks from Japanese aircraft.

The battle for Iwo Jima was characterized by brutal, close-quarters combat as American forces fought to gain control of the island. The Marines encountered numerous challenges, including rugged terrain, extensive network of caves and tunnels, and determined Japanese defenders who were prepared to fight to the death.

Thinking it would be over in a week, the United States took key sites like the airfields and Mount Suribachi early on. But they found themselves still on the island 36 days after the first landing, facing fierce resistance from Kuribayashi's men who had been given orders not to surrender. With hills that had nicknames like "The Meat Grinder," the battles turned out to be grim and bloody with a high number of casualties.

After over a month of grueling combat, American forces succeeded in capturing Iwo Jima. However, victory came at a steep cost. The battle resulted in heavy casualties on both sides, with thousands of Marines killed or wounded, along with nearly the entire defending Japanese garrison.

Although relatively small in size, the capture of Iwo Jima provided the Allies with a crucial forward base for conducting further air operations against Japan. The island served as an emergency landing site for damaged American bombers and facilitated the bombing campaign against the Japanese mainland.

AMAZING FACTS

- *The raising of the flag on Mount Suribachi,* the island's highest point, *was photographed by Joe Rosenthal, and quickly became an iconic symbol for the Marine Corps, dedicated to all those who gave their lives in military service to the United States.*
- *60% of Japanese soldiers who died in the war, died from poor nutrition.*

Iwo Jima Statue

THE ULTIMATE WEAPON – DROPPING OF THE ATOM BOMBS

The dropping of atomic bombs on Japan during World War II stands as one of the most controversial and consequential decisions in human history.

As World War II progressed, the United States and its Allies sought to bring a swift end to the conflict with Japan. However, Japan's refusal to surrender and the high casualties projected for an invasion of the Japanese home islands led American leaders to consider alternative means to force Japan to surrender.

During the war, the United States had secretly developed atomic weapons as part of the Manhattan Project. This massive scientific and engineering effort culminated in the successful creation of two atomic bombs: "Little Boy" and "Fat Man."

President Harry S. Truman, who had recently assumed office following the death of President Franklin D. Roosevelt, faced the decision of whether to use atomic weapons against Japan. Truman and his advisors weighed the potential costs of an invasion of Japan against the anticipated impact of atomic bombings on Japanese morale and the leadership's willingness to surrender.

After testing in the New Mexico desert, U.S. bombers set out for a surprise attack on August 6, where the first atomic bomb, "Little Boy," was dropped over the city of Hiroshima.

Within minutes, half the city had disappeared. The massive blast generated a shock wave and winds that flattened homes even further out. Most of the 140,000 people died because of the flash burns and intense heat that measured several million degrees Celsius, and the later effects of radiation.

Mushroom Cloud of Atom Bomb exploded over Nagasaki, Japan, on August 9, 1945.

Even after this, there was no word from the Japanese government!

Three days later, "Fat Man," the second atomic bomb was dropped on Nagasaki with the same crippling effects, killing 74,000 people from the first blast to the radioactive illnesses that claimed lives later.

The wave of heat from the bomb reached 3,000-4,000 degrees Celsius on the ground, with winds of 440 metres per second. Within half an hour, almost every building within a 1.5 mile radius was in flames. About 90% of the city's 76,000 buildings were partially or totally incinerated, or reduced to rubble.

Atomic bomb 1945 mission map (Source: Wikimedia Commons)

The atomic bombings, coupled with the Soviet Union's declaration of war against Japan, prompted Emperor Hirohito to intervene and accept the terms of unconditional surrender offered by the Allies. Japan formally surrendered on September 2, 1945, aboard the USS Missouri in Tokyo Bay, ending World War II.

The decision to use atomic bombs on Japan remains highly. Critics argue that the bombings caused unnecessary and indiscriminate acts of mass destruction, while supporters say it hastened the end of the war and saved countless lives that would have been lost in an invasion of Japan.

The atomic bombings ushered in the nuclear age and left a profound legacy of destruction, suffering, and long-term health consequences for the survivors, known as hibakusha. The events continue to serve as a poignant reminder of the devastating impact of warfare and the imperative of pursuing peace and nuclear disarmament.

AMAZING FACTS

- *Operation Meetinghouse was a little-known bomb attack that was more destructive than the atomic bombs. It was a napalm attack by the US, on March 9, 1945, that killed 100,000 people in Tokyo with many more injured.*
- *"Hiroshima Shadows" were outlines or shadows of people and objects that were burned into the ground because of the intensity of the blast of the atomic bomb dropped on that city.*
- *It took 15 years to rebuilt Nagasaki and Hiroshima.*

Tokyo, Japan, in ruins after B-29 incendiary attacks

- *The planes that dropped the atom bombs were called Enola Gay, named after the pilot's mum (Little Boy) and Bockscar (Fat Man).*
- *The Little Boy explosion was the same as blowing up 15,000 tons of TNT and sent a mushroom cloud 25,000 feet into the sky!*
- *Fat Man was even bigger – in fact 80 times more powerful, the same as 1.2 million tons of TNT!*
- *Today's nuclear missiles are 3,000 times more powerful than the atomic bombs dropped on Japan!*

SUBMARINE WARFARE – THE BATTLE FROM UNDER THE WAVES

At the outbreak of World War II, submarines were already established as formidable weapons of war. Both Allied and Axis powers recognized their potential for disrupting enemy shipping and controlling vital sea lanes. Germany, in particular, had a powerful submarine fleet, known as the U-boats, which caused havoc on Allied convoys in the Atlantic Ocean.

Submarine warfare during World War II saw significant technological advances on both sides. German U-boats were equipped with advanced torpedoes, sonar systems, and snorkels for extended underwater operations. American submarines, such as the Gato and Balao classes, were larger, faster, and better armed than their predecessors, with improved sonar and radar systems for detecting enemy targets.

The Battle of the Atlantic

The Battle of the Atlantic was one of the longest and most significant naval campaigns of World War II, spanning 1939 to 1945. It was fought primarily between the Allied powers, led by Britain and the United States, and Nazi Germany.

At the outset of the war, control of the Atlantic Ocean was crucial for the Allies to maintain supply lines (Britain imported lots of its food), transport troops, and sustain the war effort in Europe. The Axis powers wanted to disrupt these supply lines and starve Britain into submission.

1940 to 1943 saw many U-boat attacks on Allied shipping, particularly in the waters surrounding the British Isles. German U-boats operated in "wolf packs", hunting in coordinated groups to maximize their effectiveness. They targeted merchant (non-military ships) convoys bringing vital supplies to Britain, sinking numerous ships and causing heavy losses.

The Allies responded to the U-boat threat by sailing in convoys, where merchant ships were grouped together and escorted by naval vessels for protection. These convoys proved crucial in reducing losses to U-boat attacks, as the escorts provided anti-submarine protection and aerial reconnaissance.

From 1943, the Allies implemented various measures to counter the U-boat threat, including improved anti-submarine warfare tactics, technological advancements such as radar and sonar, and the introduction of long-range aircraft for maritime patrol.

By 1944, the Allies had gained the upper hand in the Battle of the Atlantic. German U-boat losses mounted, and Allied naval and air superiority made it increasingly difficult for the Axis powers to sustain their maritime offensive. The campaign effectively ended with Germany's surrender in May 1945.

The Battle of the Atlantic was a grueling and protracted struggle that resulted in a heavy toll on both sides. Thousands of ships and aircraft were lost, and tens of thousands of sailors and airmen died. However, the Allied victory in the Battle of the Atlantic played a crucial role in securing the flow of supplies to Britain and facilitating the eventual success of the Allied war effort in Europe.

The Pacific Theater

In the Pacific Ocean, submarine warfare took on a different dimension. American submarines, known as "Silent Service", played a critical role in disrupting Japanese supply lines, sinking enemy ships, and conducting reconnaissance missions. Operating in the vast expanse of the Pacific, American submarines faced unique challenges, including long supply lines and harsh environmental conditions.

American submarines, armed with torpedoes and deck guns, prowled the waters around Japan, sinking thousands of tons of enemy shipping and contributing significantly to the Allied victory in the Pacific. They targeted Japanese merchant ships, troop transports, and warships, inflicting heavy losses on the Imperial Japanese Navy.

The Battle of the Mediterranean

The Mediterranean Sea was another theater of submarine warfare, where Allied and Axis submarines clashed in a struggle for control of strategic waterways. German and Italian submarines targeted Allied convoys supplying troops in North Africa, while British submarines conducted patrols and attacks on Axis shipping.

The Battle of the Mediterranean saw numerous engagements between submarines and surface vessels, with both sides suffering losses. Allied submarines played a vital role in disrupting Axis supply lines and supporting Allied operations in North Africa and Italy.

AMAZING FACTS

- *The Allies and Axis Powers sank over 90 ships in just 8 months, in the Mediterranean in 1941!*
- *Otto Kretschmer, a German Naval Commander, sank 37 Allied ships, the most of any submariner. He was captured by the British Royal Navy in 1941.*
- *Three quarters of submariners were killed in battle. It seems a submarine was not a safe place to be!*

BATTLE OF BERLIN – THE END OF THE WAR IN EUROPE

As the war came to an end, one final act unfolded - a fierce and decisive battle for the heart of Nazi Germany, the city of Berlin. From April 16 to May 2, 1945, the Battle of Berlin raged on the streets, buildings, and skies, marking the climax of the war in Europe. This monumental struggle between the Allied forces and the defenders of the Third Reich would determine the fate of millions and shape the course of history.

Americans roll through Siegfried Line on a 'tank dozer' near Roetgen, Germany, on Sept. 28, 1944. Roetgen was the first German municipality to be captured by US troops.

After years of brutal conflict and devastating losses, the Allied forces had marched relentlessly across Europe, pushing the German army back on multiple fronts. As the Soviet Union advanced from the east, the Western Allies, including the United States, United Kingdom, and other Allied nations, closed in from the west. The fall of Berlin seemed inevitable, but the city's defenders, led by the ruthless Nazi regime of Adolf Hitler, remained determined to fight to the bitter end.

By the time the Battle of Berlin began, Allied leaders had agreed upon the division of Europe into spheres of influence, with the Western Allies focusing on the liberation of

Western Europe and the Soviets advancing into Eastern Europe. The Soviet Union was primarily responsible for the liberation of Eastern Europe and the capture of Berlin as part of this agreed-upon strategy.

The city of Cologne, Germany, after Allied bombing

The Soviet Red Army, was looking to take revenge on Germany for the suffering of the Soviet people since 1941. The fighting was brutal - the Soviets were merciless and committed many atrocities against the civilian population in retribution for German brutality earlier in the war.

The Soviet Union assembled outside Berlin one of the largest concentrations of military power ever seen. The three Soviet fronts comprised 2.5 million soldiers, 6,250 tanks,

7,500 aircraft, 41,600 artillery pieces and mortars, 3,255 truck-mounted Katyushar missile launchers (nicknamed 'Stalin organs') and 95,383 motor vehicles.

The Battle of Berlin began with a massive assault by the Soviet Red Army, the final offensive against the German capital. Soviet troops, tanks, and artillery poured across the Oder River, facing fierce resistance from the German defenders entrenched along the eastern outskirts of Berlin. The stage was set for a brutal and bloody showdown in the streets of the besieged city.

The Battle of Berlin quickly descended into a savage contest of urban warfare, as Soviet troops fought their way through the city's neighborhoods, encountering stubborn resistance from German soldiers, Hitler Youth, and fanatical Nazi Party members. The streets echoed with the thunder of artillery fire, the roar of tank engines, and the crackle of gunfire as the battle raged on day and night.

Amidst the chaos and devastation, civilians trapped in Berlin's besieged neighborhoods endured unimaginable hardships, facing shortages of food, water, and shelter as the fighting engulfed their city. Yet, amidst the despair, acts of courage and resilience emerged, as ordinary men, women, and children found strength in the face of adversity.

One of the most iconic moments of the Battle of Berlin was the storming of the Reichstag, the German parliament, by Soviet troops on April 30, 1945. As the Red Army closed in on the historic building, fierce fighting erupted between the defenders and attackers. Eventually, Soviet soldiers raised the red flag of victory atop the Reichstag, symbolizing the impending defeat of Nazi Germany.

Throughout the Battle of Berlin, Adolf Hitler remained holed up in his underground bunker beneath the Reich Chancellery, surrounded by his closest advisors and loyalists. Despite the dire situation facing Germany, Hitler refused to surrender, clinging to the delusion of victory until the very end.

The intense fighting lasted 17 days leaving 300,000 Berliners dead and 80,000 Red Army troops dead. By April 30, Hitler had finally admitted defeat by shooting himself in the head.

Five days later, General Jodl of the German army signed the unconditional surrender of Nazi Germany. The war in Europe was over.

The Battle of Berlin exacted a heavy toll on both sides, with thousands of soldiers and civilians losing their lives in the ferocious fighting. Soviet casualties were particularly high, as Red Army troops endured relentless German resistance and fierce street-to-street combat. German defenders, facing overwhelming odds and dwindling supplies, fought bravely to defend their city but ultimately succumbed to the superior firepower and numbers of the Allied forces.

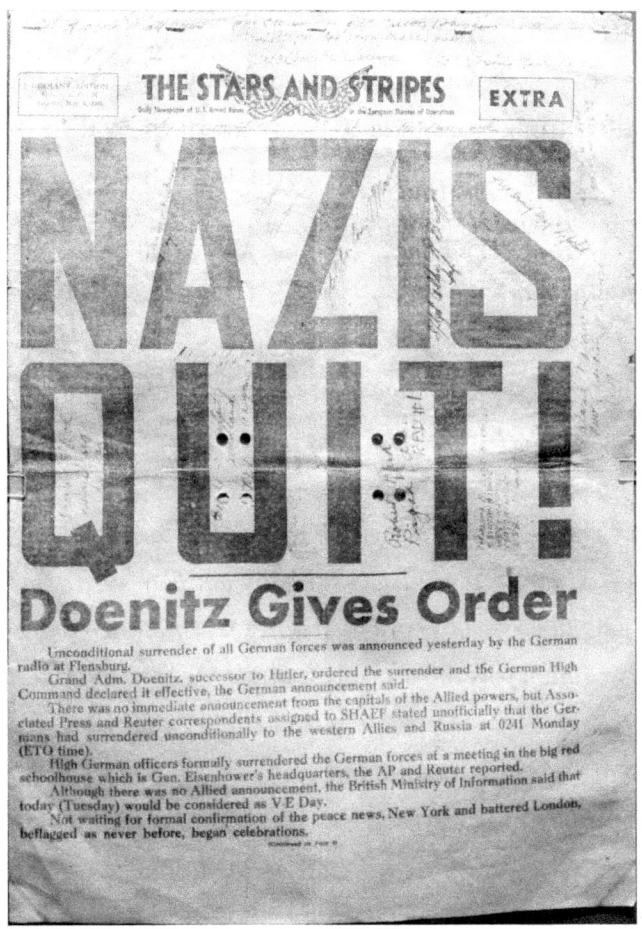

Germany Surrenders Headline

The Battle of Berlin marked the end of World War II in Europe and the collapse of the Nazi regime. The capture of Berlin by the Allied forces signaled the final defeat of Hitler's dream of a Thousand-Year Reich and the liberation of millions from tyranny and oppression.

In the aftermath of the battle, Berlin lay in ruins, a stark reminder of the devastation wrought by war. Yet, amidst the rubble and ruins, the seeds of hope and renewal took root, as the people of Berlin and the world looked towards a future of peace, freedom, and reconciliation.

AMAZING FACTS

- *Berlin's zoo was damaged, and some of the animals escaped! There were lions, tigers, and bears, walking around the city's streets!*
- *To confuse Allied intelligence and potential assassins, Adolf Hitler employed several body doubles, or doppelgangers, who bore a striking resemblance to him. These doubles were used for public appearances and other occasions to divert attention and enhance Hitler's security.*
- *27% of the built-up area of Berlin was destroyed.*
- *The propaganda minister Joseph Goebbels and his wife Magda, also committed suicide in the bunker.*
- *On April 30, Hitler married Eva Braun in his bunker, before he shot himself and Eva Braun swallowed cyanide and died. Their bodies were taken outside and burned.*

5

DARK TIMES – NAZIS AND JEWS

This chapter describes some very nasty and evil things carried out by the Nazis on Jewish people and other minority races – basically, anyone that the Germans thought was inferior to them! The Holocaust was a very dark and horrible time in history, but it's important for us to learn about it so we can make sure nothing like it ever happens again.

The Holocaust is one the worst events in history. Nazi Germany deliberated murdered 6 million Jews including 1 million children, and at least 5 million POWs, Roma Gypsies, homosexuals, disabled people, and others that Hitler hated. The hatred he encouraged against the Jews and his devious plan to get rid of them, moved him from just another dictator to someone who began a war, to a cold-blooded murderer and genocidal maniac.

(Genocide means the deliberate killing of a large number of people from a particular nation or ethnic group with the aim of destroying that nation or group.)

WHY DID THE NAZIS PERSECUTE THE JEWS?

Whether they just needed a scapegoat (someone to blame) or were truly racist, anti-Semitism (hatred of Jewish people) became one of the main beliefs of the Nazis.

It was not a secret. Hitler wrote about it shortly after WW1, in his book *Mein Kampf*, when he said, *"Its final objective must unswervingly be the removal of the Jews altogether"*. He blamed the Jews for everything; the loss of the First World War, the problems in the country, and the fact that they were rich while normal Germans starved. He painted them as people who were greedy for world domination that needed to be stopped.

Racial supremacy was what motivated Hitler and the Nazis. It was not a new idea since anti-Semitism had been around long before, but the Nazis reinvented it in a horrible new format - they turned it into mass extermination.

KRISTALLNACHT

In 1933, when Hitler came to power, many Jews lost their jobs in civil service, and their political roles. Schools limited the number of Jews in each school, and any books by Jews or Communists were burned.

On November 9, 1938, a well-planned series of attacks took place. Riots exploded and 7,500 Jewish businesses, and 1,000 synagogues were destroyed in acts of vandalism with hundreds of their windows smashed in the process, giving this event the name "Crystal Night" or Kristallnacht in German. Jewish men were rounded up and arrested, then sent off to newly built concentration camps. It was not the first time the Jews had been targeted in acts of sabotage, but it was the first coordinated violent attack. The police and firemen did nothing except make sure that other non-Jewish businesses were not damaged.

The Jews were blamed for the uprising, and as a people, were fined 1 billion Reichsmarks by Herman Goering. From that moment, Jews found they were not allowed in certain places and schools, and had their properties and goods taken from them. Their freedoms vanished.

The practice of Jews having to wear a yellow Star of David badge to show who they were came into effect in 1939. Three years later, almost every German-controlled European country had implemented the same system. Jews everywhere were being identified, and sent away.

GHETTOS

One of the problems the Nazis had was that they forced Jews out into neighboring countries, but then just as quickly, invaded those nations. Over 2 million Jews were added to the problem when Hitler invaded Poland. Part of the answer to this was to isolate these unwanted citizens by building ghettos - smaller contained suburbs within the cities. At least 30% of Poland's population was forced into 400 of these urban enclaves.

Warsaw Ghetto

People were forced to work. Restrictions were imposed on those living in these ghettos from children not being able to go to school, to a ban on religious ceremonies and holidays. The ration of food that was allowed into these neighborhoods was tiny, and many began to starve.

At any time and in different cities, Jews would be rounded up, taken out, forced to dig large graves, and then shot. These mass shootings were widespread and were the main method of killing by the Einsatzgruppen, the group of men moving through Russia with the German army.

But the ghettos were not just to keep the Jews in one place, they were also created as temporary confines until they could be moved to their final destination: extermination camps.

CONCENTRATION CAMPS

Six camps had been built in Poland especially for the purpose of killing large groups of people at a time, mainly Jews. These were at Treblinka, Auschwitz-Birkenau, Belzec, Chelmno, Majdanek, and Sobibor.

Children at Auschwitz

Prisoners were squashed into freight car trains to be transported on long journeys to the camps with hardly any water, food, or air. Many died along the way from starvation, dehydration, or suffocation. On arrival, a doctor would select those who were sick, very young, old, or pregnant to be processed first, and they were led directly to the gas chambers to be killed.

The rest were allocated colored triangles on their uniforms depending on their status; red meant political prisoners, purple was for Jehovah's Witnesses, green and black for criminals, homosexuals were given pink, while Jews had two yellow triangles overlapping to form the Star of David. At Auschwitz, all detainees were tattooed with a number to keep track of the prisoners.

Auschwitz Camp

Those who were seen as fit enough were forced to work, often dying from exhaustion, excessive beatings from the guards, malnutrition, or disease before they even reached the gas chambers. The average length of time in a camp that a prisoner stayed alive was just three months!

Most died in the gas chambers. This was known by the Nazis as the "Final Solution." Large groups were herded into a room where they were ordered to remove all their clothes and possessions before entering what they were told were "showers." The doors were shut, and carbon monoxide pumped in, or Zyklon-B pellets (a cyanide-based poison) thrown in. It took up to 20 minutes for all two thousand in the chamber to die.

Getting rid of the bodies caused another problem for the Nazis as there were so many. Groups of Jewish prisoners were made to remove everything from the dead bodies including hair, tooth fillings, jewelry and artificial limbs, before the corpses were buried in deep pits. Later, Himmler ordered huge crematoria to be built at the camps for quicker disposal, so the bodies could be burned. The concentration camps operated like factories, receiving people, killing them, and disposing of the remains as efficiently as possible with the least amount of cost. Between 4,000 and 8,000 people were burned each day.

In total, 6 million Jews were killed during the Nazi's reign, with over 3 million exterminated in these camps. That was about a third of all the Jews in the world at that time.

AMAZING FACTS

- *In 1940, Adolf Eichmann, as Nazi SS official suggested a plan to expel all Jews to the island of Madagascar off the African coast. They even though about sending them to Russia!*

ANNE FRANK

The history of the Holocaust would not be complete without the diaries of Anne Frank.

This book tells the story of a girl and her family that moved to the Netherlands when Hitler came to power in Germany. They had to hide after the Germans invaded the Netherlands and began rounding up Jews. They were discovered after two years and sent off to Auschwitz where they were split up as a family. Anne and her mother eventually died from disease.

Otto Frank, her father, returned after the war, found the diary, and published it in 1947. It's one of the closest writings we have of the terror and horror that Jews faced during that time.

THE END AND AFTERMATH

When the Allies finally defeated the Nazi army, and Hitler committed suicide, the Holocaust ended as well. But the pain and hardship did not end there.

When the Allied soldiers reached the camps, they were shocked by what they found. They discovered starving prisoners, many on the brink of death, as well as mass graves, crematoria, and evidence of systematic genocide. The survivors were in desperate need of medical attention, food, and care after enduring unimaginable suffering and deprivation.

Special diets for prisoners typically included nutrient-rich foods such as soups, broths, high-protein foods, vegetables, fruits, and fortified beverages.

Medical care, and psychological support were given to help survivors reintegrate into society and rebuild their lives after the trauma of the Holocaust. Many survivors faced ongoing health challenges and psychological scars as a result of their experiences in the concentration camps, and the process of recovery was long and difficult for many.

Around 7 to 9 million people had been displaced or moved out of their original countries. Most of these returned but others refused. Life could not be normal again going back to places where they had been hunted and tortured.

The pressure to create a homeland for the Jewish people was one of the main reasons the State of Israel was established in May 1948, and Jewish refugees were allowed to move there. But the issue of the concentration camps still posed a problem—the atrocities were so shocking, and against humane law that those involved had to be brought to justice and punished.

The Nuremberg Trials in 1945 – 1946, tried 22 Nazi officials for different war crimes, among them were the events at the camps. Others like Einsatzgruppen members, commanders, and German generals were also charged, but many escaped or had already committed suicide.

- The Nuremberg Trials were the first to use the word 'genocide' to mean the systematic murder of a group of people based on shared characteristics such as race.
- The trials were the first to convict people of 'crimes against humanity' – atrocities so bad that they damaged the whole human race.

Units were setup by the Allies to investigate and gather evidence of war crimes and locate the perpetrators. Many Nazi war criminals fled Europe after the war, seeking refuge in countries around the world. Allied governments pursued extradition requests to bring these individuals to trial.

Other trials took place in the following decades, as Nazi leaders were tracked down and found:

- In 1961, Adolf Eichmann who supervised the train transport to the camps was tried in Jerusalem, after escaping Germany to Argentina.
- In 1987, Klaus Barbie, known as 'The Butcher of Lyon' (Lyon is in France) was tried in court and

sentenced to life in prison, for ordering Jews to be killed.
- In 1998, Maurice Papon was put on trial for deporting 1,600 Jews from France.
- In 2022, at 101 years of age, Josef Schütz was the oldest person ever to stand trial for crimes committed by the Nazi regime, charged with helping in the murder of 3,518 prisoners.

No matter how many years have passed, justice finally caught up with these evil people.

Though up to a million people are believed to have actively participated in the extermination of millions of Jewish people during the Holocaust, only around 20,000 were ever found guilty of crimes, and fewer than 600 received heavy prison sentences.

What shocked the world the most was the extent of the genocide that took place, and how well-organized it all was. It was a cleansing of Jews from the Third Reich.

6

SECRET MISSIONS, SPIES AND CODE BREAKERS

Everyone loves a secret mission and in World War II there were plenty, all designed to gather intelligence, to sabotage enemy operations or for spying. Most were sensible and involved very brave people risking their lives, and others were simply crazy! Let's take a look at some of these missions.

SECRET MISSIONS

Operation Mincemeat

This was a successful British mission, designed to fool the Germans into thinking the Allies would invade Sardinia and Greece instead of Sicily.

The idea was thought up by Ian Fleming, who later wrote the James Bond books! The body of a dead tramp called

Glyndwr Michael was dressed up as a British officer called William Martin. In his pockets were documents detailing the plan to invade Sardinia and Greece. His body was transported by submarine and released near the Spanish coast. It was found by a fisherman and the documents passed on to the Germans, who believed everything they read, and moved their troops away from Sicily.

The plan worked so well that the Nazis were still expecting the attacks in Sardinia and Greece, even while they were fighting in Sicily! The plan helped the Allies conquer Sicily in 5 weeks and then advance into mainland Italy.

Operation Jedburgh

This operation was planned to support the D-Day invasion of France. Teams of three soldiers, one each from the United States, United Kingdom, and France, were dropped behind enemy lines in Nazi-occupied France to support attacks on enemy lines of communication and infrastructure, diverting German soldiers and resources away from the battlefront. They also reported on German troop movements and organised local resistance groups. The motto of the group was "Surprise, Kill, Vanish".

Operation Gunnerside

In February 1943, Hitler's development of an atomic bomb was sabotaged by a small team of soldiers. Now known as the Heroes of Telemark, these Norwegian commandoes carried out one of the most important and daring missions in World War II history - a suicide mission that they all survived.

By invading Norway, Germany gained access to a supply of heavy water – a key ingredient in building an atom bomb! The Telemark heroes battled cold, snow and treacherous mountains for several days, to achieve what was thought impossible – to get into the plant unseen, destroy the plant with no civilian casualties, and then escape alive! The mission was a success and demonstrated the effectiveness of sabotage operations and the role of resistance fighters in the war. Very brave and hardy people indeed!

Operation Fortitude

In 1944, the Germans knew the Allies would launch an invasion across The English Channel – they just didn't know where or when it would happen. Operation Fortitude was designed to fool the Germans into thinking the Allies would invade France at Calais and not Normandy.

A made-up army was created called the First United State Army Group (FUSAG) under the command of General Patton – he was the senior American commander and chosen to make it appear to the Germans that FUSAG was real. Then around Dover and the south-east of England, fake landing craft, inflatable tanks, planes and fake vehicles were positioned, which when viewed from the air looked real to the Germans, suggesting a Calais invasion.

Fake radio messages were transmitted to make the Germans think the invasion would happen at Calais in mid-July 1944 and double agents also gave fake information to the Germans.

The operation was successful, and widely regarded as one of the most successful deception operations in military history. The Germans delayed sending reinforcements to Normandy even after D-Day, still convinced the Allies were landing in Calais!

Operation Pastorius

It wasn't just the Allies with secret missions – this was a German plan to sabotage the production of war materials in the United States, specifically targeting aluminum and magnesium plants.

Eight German agents were landed on Long Island and Florida in June 1942, but the plan quickly failed after two of the agents, George John Dasch and Ernest Peter Burger, defected to the Federal Bureau of Investigation shortly after being deployed, and betrayed the other six.

Operation Halyard

This was the greatest rescue mission of World War II, saving 513 American and other Allied airmen, trapped behind enemy lines in Serbia.

Over 20,000 bombing missions were carried out over Romanian oil fields, with 50% of the aircraft involved being shot down. Local Serbian farmers and peasants risked their own lives to give refuge and food to the airmen that survived. In 1944, Operation Halyard was launched. American agents of Serbian descent were sent behind enemy lines to gather the American airmen and organise the evacuation. The risks were huge - a landing strip large enough for cargo planes had to be made, without alerting the Germans – so they worked mostly at night.

The risk to the cargo planes was huge - not only entering enemy territory without being shot down, but also landing, retrieving the airmen, then taking off and flying out of that same territory, again without being shot down. Despite this, the rescue was a complete success, but received little to no publicity.

Operation Eiche

This was a daring German operation to rescue the former Italian leader Mussolini. After the Allies invaded Italy, Mussolini had been expelled from office and held in a hotel in a remote mountain ski resort.

There was no easy way to reach the hotel from the ground. Waffen SS officer Otto Skorzeny, decided to risk an attack in 12 gliders, landing on the mountain in silence and easily overpowering Mussolini's guards. Mussolini was led to safety in Austria before being killed in April 1945.

SPIES AND RESISTANCE FIGHTERS

Amidst the chaos and devastation, there emerged individuals who played crucial roles in shaping the course of history. Among these were the spies and resistance fighters, whose daring exploits and unwavering courage became legendary.

Imagine a world where secrets held the power to change the fate of nations, where danger lurked around every corner, and every whisper could mean the difference between victory and defeat. In this world of espionage and clandestine operations, spies became the unsung heroes, operating in the shadows to gather intelligence, sabotage enemy efforts, and turn the tide of war.

But it wasn't just professional spies who made a difference. Across occupied territories, ordinary men and women rose up to resist oppression and fight against tyranny. These brave people formed underground networks, risking their lives to sabotage enemy infrastructure, smuggle vital supplies, and provide shelter and aid to those in need. They became the heart and soul of the resistance movements that defied Nazi occupation and inspired hope in the darkest of times.

Let's look at some of these brave heroes.

Virginia Hall: Allied Spy

Codenamed Marie, but known as the "Limping Lady," due to her wooden leg (which she called Cuthbert!), Hall was one of the most hunted spies by the Nazis. Working undercover in France, she organized routes, supplies, and information through an extensive spy network that she helped to set up. By 1943, her British organizers realized that it was too dangerous for her to continue, and they pulled her out.

But the Americans saw her as an asset, and sent her back where she continued her work, even encouraging a group of partisans called the Marquis to resist the Nazis by supplying them with weapons. At one point, she escaped to Spain by climbing across the Pyrenees through heavy snow, despite her 8lbs (4kg) wooden leg!

She was awarded the Distinguished Service Cross, and later worked for the CIA.

Nancy Wake: Guerrilla Fighter

Codenamed "The White Mouse," she worked with Marquis groups, even taking command of the rough men at times. At one stage, she traveled hundreds of miles on her own to make radio contact when their communication lines were down. Her ability to organize and get the job done earned her the respect of all those around her, whether it was shooting Nazis or blowing up buildings. She once killed an SS sentry with her bare hands.

She was awarded numerous awards from America, Britain, and France.

Noor Inayat Khan: British Spy

Khan was of Indian descent and codenamed Madeleine. She worked as a radio operator in Nazi-occupied France, evading capture for several months, but she was hunted by the Gestapo as they knew about her and what she had been doing, but not who she was.

She stayed in France, despite the arrests of those around her, as she saw the work as too important. She was the lone radio operator for four months in Paris until she was betrayed by a double agent and handed over to the Gestapo who tried in vain to get information from her.

She was sent to Berlin, but even there, despite torture, she remained loyal to the cause. On September 12, 1944, she was executed.

Eileen Nearne: British Spy

In France in 1944, Nearne worked with a network called "The Wizard" that sent over 100 secret messages back to England. To avoid being caught, she moved often and was always very careful, but the German secret police found her in a raid. She managed to destroy all the evidence, but she suffered incredible torture as the Nazis suspected her of espionage.

She never gave in, sticking to her story that she was a French secretary. Sent to many concentration camps, she managed to escape and hide in a church in Leipzig until the Allies freed the country. Nearne died in 2010, and her wartime exploits were only revealed after a search of her apartment uncovered her war medals. She was then given a hero's funeral.

Roald Dahl, the famous British author: British Spy

Before he became famous for writing books such as "Charlie and the Chocolate Factory" and "James and the Giant Peach," Dahl was part of a British spy ring in Washington, D.C. He joined the Royal Air Force in 1939 and trained as a fighter pilot. He flew a number of combat missions before injuries suffered during a crash-landing in the North African desert ended his military flying career.

In 1942, Dahl was appointed assistant air attaché at the British embassy in Washington, where he was recruited to join a spy network called the British Security Coordination (BSC). The group, whose members included future James Bond creator Ian Fleming, was tasked with planting propaganda and carrying out other covert activities designed to persuade a reluctant United States to join the war against Germany.

In his role as an undercover agent, Dahl gathered intelligence about the U.S. political scene by befriending the capital's movers and shakers, including politicians, journalists, corporate tycoons, socialites and even first lady Eleanor Roosevelt.

Juan Pujol García

Codenamed Garbo, Garcia was a Spanish double agent who worked for the British and one of the most important secret agents of the Second World War. He fed misinformation to the Germans, which diverted German forces away from the Normandy landing, which was crucial to the success of the D-Day invasion.

His deception was so convincing that the Germans continued to believe in Pujol throughout the war – six weeks after D-Day Hitler awarded him the Iron Cross for his 'extraordinary services'. Pujol received an MBE from the British in December 1944, although in secret to avoid exposing him.

Richard Sorge

Sorge was a Soviet spy who worked undercover in Nazi Germany and Imperial Japan, speaking to the leading politicians and generals. He provided valuable information to the Soviets, regarding Operation Barbarossa and Japanese intentions not to invade Siberia in 1941 proved pivotal to the Soviet counteroffensive in the Battle of Moscow.

Dusko Popov

Codenamed Tricycle, Dusko Popov was a Serbian double agent who worked for both the British MI6 and the German Abwehr. He provided valuable intelligence to the Allies while also misleading the Germans, again about the D-Day landings, keeping seven German divisions at Pas de Calais for three weeks after the Allies landed in Normandy. He is said to be the inspiration for James Bond!

AMAZING FACTS

- *Posters were displayed across Britain, with messages such as 'Careless talk costs lives!" and " Walls have ears!". These messages were a warning that German spies could be lurking anywhere, eavesdropping and passing on intelligence to the Nazis.*

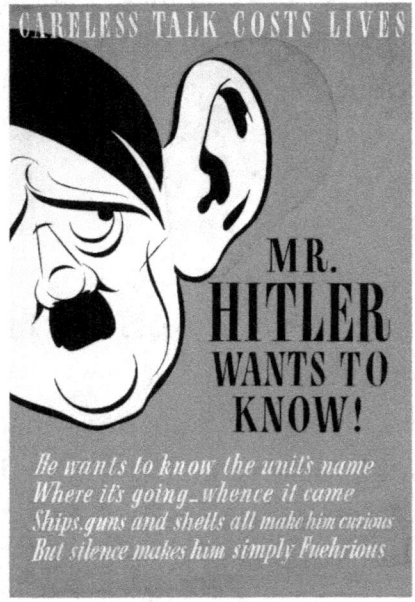

Careless talk costs lives poster

SCIENTISTS

Scientists and their discoveries and innovations changed the course of history. From unlocking the secrets of the atom to developing life-saving medicines, these brilliant individuals played a crucial role in shaping the outcome of the war.

They became soldiers in their own right, using their knowledge and expertise to tackle the challenges of war head-on.

Physicists unlocked the power of the atom, chemists developed life-saving medicines, engineers built revolutionary weapons, and mathematicians cracked codes and solved puzzles that helped win the war.

Their work not only helped secure victory for their nations but also laid the foundation for the technological advancements that would shape the world in the years to come.

Alan Turing

Alan Turing was a British mathematician and computer scientist, and the superhero of code-breaking. During the war, the Germans were sending secret messages using a code called the Enigma machine. It was like a super complicated puzzle with trillions of possible combinations.

But Alan Turing was up for the challenge of breaking the German code. He worked with a team of codebreakers at a top-secret place called Bletchley Park in England. They built a machine called the Bombe, which was like a super-fast computer that could help crack the Enigma code.

Turing was a genius when it came to figuring out patterns and solving puzzles. He came up with all sorts of clever tricks and techniques to break the code faster. And guess what? He did it! He helped crack the Enigma code, which was a huge deal because it meant that the Allies could read the enemy's secret messages and know what they were up to. And the Germans didn't know their messages could be read and continued to send them.

Devising a machine that could break the Enigma code, allowed the British to have access to up to 84,000 messages intended for the Nazis every month. It was this breakthrough that gave the Allies the upper hand, being able to know Hitler's plans beforehand. It's thought his work helped to shorten the war by 2–3 years, saving thousands if not millions of lives.

But Turing didn't stop there. He also helped invent something called the Turing machine, which is like the granddaddy of all computers. His ideas laid the foundation for modern computers and artificial intelligence, which we use every day.

He is remembered as one of the greatest minds of his time and a true hero of World War II.

Joan Clarke

Part of the group that cracked the Enigma code, Clarke's brilliance in mathematics gave her a unique advantage in seeing patterns and formulas. This insight gave her the unique ability to be a cryptanalyst, and she worked closely with Alan Turing. She continued to work for the government as a code breaker long after the war.

Jane Hughes Fawcett

Another code breaker, Fawcett was credited for sinking the German battleship Bismarck. On May 25, 1941, she caught the message of where the Nazi's newest warship was headed, giving the Allies the directions to attack. The next day they tracked the elusive Bismarck and sank her.

Jane and Joan are just two of the women of Bletchley Park, where over 8,000 worked including many cryptanalysts. Few received any credit for their work, and many never revealed their work even later in life.

Barnes Wallis

Barnes Wallis was a British engineer, and he was like the Tony Stark of his time – super inventive and always thinking outside the box.

One of his most famous inventions was something called the "bouncing bomb". This wasn't just any ordinary bomb. Barnes Wallis figured out that if you dropped a bomb in just the right way, it could skip across the surface of the water like a stone and then sink right next to an enemy target, such as a dam or a bridge.

So, he designed these special bombs that were round and had a spinning mechanism inside. When they were dropped from a plane at just the right height and speed, they would bounce along the water and hit their target perfectly.

Coming up with the idea was just the beginning. Barnes Wallis had to convince a lot of people that his bouncing bomb could actually work. He had to do lots of tests and experiments to prove that it was possible.

And it worked! The bouncing bomb became a crucial weapon for the British during the war. They used it in a daring mission called the "Dam Busters raid," where they flew low over enemy territory and dropped the bombs on important German dams, causing huge floods and disrupting their war efforts.

But Barnes Wallis didn't stop there. He also invented other cool stuff, like the "Tallboy" bomb, which was a giant bomb that could destroy really tough targets, like underground bunkers.

Barnes Wallis was like the ultimate inventor-hero of World War II. He used his genius and creativity to come up with game-changing inventions that helped his country win the war. And even though he's not as famous as some other war heroes, his contributions were absolutely crucial in the fight against the Nazis.

J. Robert Oppenheimer

Oppenheimer and his team led the Manhattan Project, and were given a crucial mission by the United States government. Their job? To build a top-secret weapon, called an atomic bomb, before the Germans could.

Building an atomic bomb wasn't like building a model airplane or baking cookies. It was incredibly complicated and required a lot of brainpower and hard work. Oppenheimer and his team had to figure out how to split tiny particles called atoms to release a huge amount of energy – like unlocking a super powerful energy source.

They worked day and night in secret labs, solving tricky problems and testing new ideas. And finally, after lots of trial and error, they did it, building the the world's first atomic bomb.

Oppenheimer was a very smart guy, and he knew that this bomb wasn't just a great invention – it was also really very dangerous. He felt a mix of pride for what they had achieved and concern about what it meant for the world.

When the bomb was ready, it was used help end the war quicker. But after seeing the devastation it caused, Oppenheimer felt a deep sense of responsibility. He realized that with great power comes great responsibility, and he spent the rest of his life working for peace and trying to make sure that something like this never happened again.

Reginald Jones

Reginald Victor Jones was a British scientist and intelligence officer, and he played a really important role in helping his country win the war. The British were worried about the

Germans using airplanes to drop bombs on cities and cause a lot of destruction.

But Jones wasn't about to let that happen without a fight. He used his skills in science and technology to come up with all sorts of clever tricks and tactics to foil the enemy's plans.

One of his biggest achievements was figuring out how to jam the radar systems that the Germans used to guide their airplanes. Radar was like their secret weapon, helping them find their targets even in the dark or bad weather. But Jones and his team developed special devices that could send out signals to mess up the enemy's radar, making it harder for them to find their targets.

Jones also played a key role in something called "Operation Bodyguard," which was a massive deception campaign to trick the Germans about where the Allies were going to attack. He used his knowledge of science and psychology to come up with all sorts of creative ways to fool the enemy and keep them guessing.

Thanks to Jones's cleverness and quick thinking, the Allies were able to gain the upper hand and eventually win the war. His work helped save countless lives and made a huge difference in the outcome of World War II.

7

TECH AND GADGETS

This chapter is all about the inventions that came to life during wartime as each side tried to gain an advantage over the other, and some inventions that were so mad they were never used!

But let's start with something more basic, but important – kit and food!

KIT

Soldiers carried much of their kit around with them. British soldiers were given clothes, boots, weapons and a personal kit. They carried a water-bottle, ammunition pouches, entrenching tool (spade), a groundsheet and a haversack containing a mess-tin, tinned rations, extra iron rations, spare socks and laces.

American soldiers who landed in France on D-Day, didn't know when they would be resupplied, so they each carried a huge amount of supplies with their backpacks weighing 70-100 pounds (30-45kg)!

AMAZING FACTS

- *Russian soldiers didn't have socks. Yes, fighting in the cold of a Russian winter, instead of socks, they wrapped their feet in square cloths (called Portyanki)! These footwraps were used in the Russian army until 2013. They were only changed weekly - imagine the smell!*

FOOD

British soldiers, whenever possible were served fresh, hot food, but those on the front line or on the move, were given preserved foods. At the start of the war, this included tinned corned beef, M&V which was a meat and vegetable stew and service biscuits, which were unsalted, hard and dry. They had little flavour and soldiers soaked them in water or tea to make them chewable.

The Germans had rations of hard bread and canned meat along with soup.

Early in the war, Soviet troops fought on minimal rations, and were expected to find food wherever they were fighting. They particularly liked the rations of captured German soldiers, and often raids would be planned around capture of supply dumps containing foodstuffs.

Towards the end of the war, with food in short supply, the Russians made carrot tea by grating carrots and boiling it with tree fungus! Russian submariners were given extra rations including red wine, sauerkraut, cucumber and raw onions to prevent scurvy and to compensate for the lack of oxygen.

The American soldiers probably had the best rations. Their K-rations included canned chopped eggs, dried fruit, canned meat, cigarettes, coffee, cheese, chewing gum and chocolate.

WEAPONS

When it comes to weapons, the British infantry used the same weapon as they had in World War 1, the Lee Enfield, which had a magazine of 10 rounds. After each shot, the gun's 'bolt' had to be pulled back to remove the fired shell and to load another. Despite this, a British soldier could fire 15 shots a minute! The British also used the Sten gun, a submachine that was cheap to produce. It could fire 550 rounds per minute, but often jammed if more than 30 rounds were loaded!

The Americans had the M1 Garand, which was semi-automatic, meaning it could fire repeatedly without the soldier having to eject the shell manually after each shot. They also had the Tommy gun, a submachine gun used in WW1 and also the Browning Automatic Refile, accurate to 1,500 yards and able to fire 600 rounds per minute.

For the Germans, the standard issues rifle was the Mauser 98k, which dated back to 1898. It could only be loaded with 5 rounds, limiting the firepower of the soldiers, but it was a very accurate and reliable weapon. 15 million were produced between 1935 and 1945.

The Russians used the Mosin-Nagant, one of the most mass-produced guns ever. It was also used by Russian snipers. The Finnish version of the gun was used by Simo Häyhä, considered the deadliest sniper in history. All his kills were Soviets, so the Russian Army was probably not too happy about that!

TECHNOLOGY

Now let's delve into the more exciting tech that was invented and sometimes used in the war −some inventions were so mad that they were never used! From faster planes to secret spy gadgets, the war sparked a wave of innovation.

The need for superior weapons and supplies during the war had pushed both the Allies and the Axis Powers to invest heavily in research. The result was impressive and proved to be a massive leap forward in technology for the entire world.

The Nazis brought out cutting-edge equipment that could have won them the war if they had had more time to refine and produce these products. The V2 rocket and jet engines were among their top achievements.

Radar played a massive role in the Battle of the Atlantic, other sea skirmishes, and air battles, and would later be used to track civilian planes and storms. The birth of the computer, one of the biggest breakthroughs of the 20th century, was a result of Alan Turing and other inventors' innovative ideas.

Huge scientific advances were made in medicine. The first flu vaccine was used in the United States in 1945, and penicillin, which had been discovered in 1928, was widely produced for troops. Even blood transfusions were formulated by Charles Drew for the military.

Enigma Machine

The Enigma Machine was a sophisticated encryption device used by the German military to encode messages so even if intercepted by the enemy, the messages couldn't be understood. British mathematician and computer scientist Alan Turing and his team at Bletchley Park successfully deciphered Enigma-encoded messages, providing the Allies with crucial intelligence.

Miniature Cameras

Miniature cameras, often concealed in everyday objects like pens or cigarette cases, were used by spies to discreetly capture photographs of documents, maps, and other sensitive information.

Microdots

Microdots were tiny photographs reduced to the size of a punctuation mark. They were often used to conceal messages within other documents or objects and required a magnifying glass to be deciphered.

Invisible Ink

Invisible ink, made from substances like lemon juice or milk, allowed spies to write messages that were initially invisible and could be revealed later using heat or chemicals.

Glider and Parachute Espionage

Both the Allies and the Axis powers developed gliders and parachute techniques for covert insertions of agents into enemy territory. These allowed spies to conduct sabotage, gather intelligence, and assist resistance movements.

OSS X-2 Camera

The Office of Strategic Services (OSS), later the CIA, developed the X-2 camera, a compact and quiet camera used for clandestine photography. It played a role in intelligence gathering and covert operations.

Silenced Weapons

Silenced pistols and submachine guns were developed to allow spies and special forces to kill their targets quietly and without attracting attention.

Bouncing Bomb

Developed by Sir Barnes Wallace and the Royal Air Force (RAF), bouncing bombs were designed to skip across the surface of the water before striking a target. They were famously used in the "Dam Busters" raid to bomb German dams and damage the manufacturing industry of the Germans.

Limpet Mines

Limpet mines were magnetic explosive devices attached to the hulls of enemy ships by underwater swimmers or frogmen. They were used for sabotage and covert naval operations.

Atom Bombs

As we've seen in the previous chapter, there was a huge advance in harnessing atomic energy. They figured out how to use it to create a super powerful bomb, known as the atom bomb. It was so strong that it changed the course of the war in the Pacific.

But wait, there's more to this story. The atom bomb was so powerful that it made everyone realize how important it was to use science for good things, not just for war. It led to countries to work together to make sure such powerful weapons were used responsibly, or better still, not at all!

While many innovations played important roles in the war, not all were put into use. Let's look at some of the mad World War II inventions that were never widely used.

Bat Bombs

Invented by American dentist Lytle S. Adams, the idea was to attach incendiary devices (designed to cause fires) to bats and release them over Japanese cities. The bats would roost in buildings, and then the incendiaries would ignite, causing widespread fires. The project, known as Project X-Ray, was tested but never used.

The Great Panjandrum

An enormous, rocket-propelled wheel with explosive charges, designed to roll across the water and onto enemy beaches, detonating mines and other obstacles. The British military tested it in 1944, but it proved uncontrollable and impractical.

Project Pigeon (Project Orcon)

This project aimed to use trained pigeons to guide bombs to their targets. The pigeons, housed in the nose of the bomb, were trained to peck at images on a screen, guiding the bomb toward the intended target. The project was abandoned in favor of more reliable guidance systems.

Jet Pack Infantry

Various nations experimented with the idea of equipping soldiers with jet packs for rapid mobility on the battlefield.

While jet packs have been developed for various purposes, they were not extensively used in World War II.

The Bat-Plane

The bat-plane was a concept for a stealthy aircraft designed to resemble a bat. The idea was that enemy radar would mistake it for a flock of birds, allowing it to approach undetected. The concept did not progress beyond the design stage.

The Windkanone (Wind Cannon)

Proposed by the Germans, the Windkanone was a massive cannon designed to shoot a vortex of air at enemy aircraft, disrupting their flight and causing them to crash. The concept was abandoned due to its impracticality.

AIRCRAFT

Control of the skies was crucial in World War 2, and all sides developed new aircraft and continued to make improvements throughout the war.

Britain

The British Royal Air Force (RAF) operated a wide range of aircraft, playing a crucial role in both the defense of Britain and in offensive operations against Axis powers.

Supermarine Spitfire

The Spitfire was a symbol of British air power during the Battle of Britain. Its agility and speed, combined with excellent handling, made it a formidable adversary against German fighters. It played a crucial role in defending British airspace and achieving air superiority.

Hawker Hurricane

Another important fighter aircraft used by the RAF during the Battle of Britain. The Hurricane was rugged and reliable, and while it was not as fast or manoeuvrable as the Spitfire, it was highly effective in combat.

Avro Lancaster

The Lancaster was a four-engine heavy bomber used by the RAF in night bombing raids over Germany. 7,377 were built during the war. It played a vital role in the British Bomber Command's efforts to undermine German industry and morale.

United States

US aircraft included fighters, bombers, helicopters and carrier-based fighters.

North American P-51 Mustang

The P-51 Mustang became one of the most successful and versatile fighter aircraft of the war. Its long-range capabilities, coupled with a powerful Rolls-Royce Merlin engine, made it an effective escort fighter for American bombers during strategic bombing raids over Europe.

Boeing B-17 Flying Fortress

The B-17 was a heavy bomber used by the U.S. Army Air Forces for strategic bombing campaigns in Europe. It became iconic for its ability to absorb damage and still return its crew safely, contributing to the daylight bombing strategy.

Douglas C-47 Skytrain

The C-47 was a military transport aircraft used extensively by the Allies for airborne operations, including the D-Day landings and Operation Market Garden. It played a crucial role in transporting troops and supplies.

Sikorsky R-4

The R-4 was the world's first mass-produced helicopter and played a role in air-sea rescue missions during the war. Its development marked the early stages of rotary-wing aircraft in military operations.

Grumman F6F Hellcat

A carrier-based fighter aircraft used by the United States Navy and Marine Corps in the Pacific. The Hellcat was highly successful in aerial combat against Japanese aircraft and played a key role in achieving air superiority over the Pacific.

Grumman TBF Avenger

A torpedo bomber used by the U.S. Navy and Marine Corps for anti-submarine warfare, bombing, and reconnaissance missions. The Avenger played a crucial role in sinking enemy ships and submarines in the Pacific war.

Douglas SBD Dauntless

A dive bomber used by the U.S. Navy and Marine Corps in the Pacific. The Dauntless played a significant role in the Battle of Midway, where its attacks contributed to the destruction of several Japanese aircraft carriers.

Lockheed P-38 Lightning

A unique twin-engine fighter known for its distinctive twin-boom design and versatility. The P-38 served in various roles, including interception, dive bombing, and reconnaissance, and saw action in both the Europe and Pacific.

Germany

Germany had fighters and bombers but also the world's first operational jet-powered fighter aircraft.

Messerschmitt Bf 109

The Bf 109 was the primary German fighter throughout the war. It was a versatile and heavily armed aircraft, playing a key role in the early Blitzkrieg campaigns and the Battle of Britain. It remained in service throughout the war and was one of the most produced fighter aircraft in history.

Focke-Wulf Fw 190

The Fw 190 was a highly effective German fighter that excelled in air-to-air combat. It complemented the Bf 109 and was particularly successful on the Eastern Front against Soviet aircraft.

Junkers Ju 87 Stuka

The Stuka was a German dive bomber that played a key role in the early Blitzkrieg campaigns. Its distinctive sirens, used during dives, had a psychological impact on enemy forces. However, it became vulnerable in the face of more advanced fighter planes later in the war.

Heinkel He 111

A medium bomber used by the Luftwaffe in various roles, including strategic bombing, tactical bombing, and maritime patrol. The He 111 was one of the most widely used bombers in the German arsenal and saw extensive service throughout the war.

Messerschmitt Me 262

The world's first operational jet-powered fighter aircraft, the Me 262 represented a significant technological advancement for the Luftwaffe. Although introduced late in the war, it demonstrated exceptional speed and performance but was hampered by production issues and fuel shortages.

Japan

Mitsubishi A6M Zero

The Zero was the primary Japanese carrier-based fighter at the beginning of the war. Its agility and long range contributed to early Japanese successes in the Pacific. However, it became outclassed by more advanced Allied aircraft as the war progressed.

Nakajima B5N

A carrier-based torpedo bomber used by the Imperial Japanese Navy (IJN) in various naval operations. The B5N, also known as the "Kate," was instrumental in the attack on Pearl Harbor and was used in subsequent battles across the Pacific.

Aichi D3A

A dive bomber used by the IJN in the Pacific Theater. The D3A, known as the "Val," was deployed in the early stages of the war and played a key role in attacks on Allied ships and installations.

Mitsubishi G4M

A twin-engine bomber used by the IJN for long-range bombing missions. The G4M, also known as the "Betty," was utilized in attacks on Allied ships, islands, and mainland targets.

In World War II, technology wasn't just about machines; it was about brilliant minds coming together to invent things that could make a difference. The war might have been a tough time, but the inventions and innovations that came out of it have shaped the way we live today. So, let's salute the clever inventors who turned wartime challenges into awesome solutions!

8

PRISONERS OF WAR (POWS)

Let's look at what happened to prisoners of war and the different ways in which they were treated by the different sides in the war. Over 94,000 Americans with imprisoned as POWs in Europe, and 170,000 British soldiers – all of these men had to be housed and fed, so you can imagine the effort this involved.

When enemy soldiers are captured, international law is clear that any prisoner of war has certain rights and access to medical and humane treatment regardless of their nationality. But in WW2, these laws were often ignored, especially in German and Japanese camps where POWs were given little food, tortured, and exposed to the point of death. The horrific conditions that they endured were some of the worst atrocities during the war.

GERMANY

For the most part, when it came to the Allies, Germany stuck to the Geneva Convention terms, treating the prisoners as well as could be expected under the conditions. Only the name, rank, and serial number were required when POWs gave their details, but officers did their best to try and trick extra information out of them.

German POW camps were called *Stalags* and were located throughout Nazi-occupied countries. Once prisoners arrived by train, they would receive two meals of thin soup and bread each day, although this became much less as German supplies ran out.

Red Cross parcels were allowed with luxury items of chocolate, biscuits, and other things. Men were housed in wooden barracks stacked with bunk beds and a central coal stove. Some worked, but the biggest drawbacks were hunger and boredom.

The Russians did not enjoy the same treatment. They were given below the daily ration of food or starved, resulting in 5,000 deaths a day. This number increased when winter set in.

Instead of giving medical treatment, the Nazis solved the problem by removing the wounded Russians and shooting them. Over 65,000 were starved in the Gross-Rosen camp, others were burned alive in Flossenburg, while in Majdanek and Mauthausen countless were shot. By the beginning of 1942, 2 million Soviet POWs had died.

AMAZING FACTS

- *A British soldier escaped to see his German girlfriend and came back to the camp he was at over 200 times without guards ever knowing.*
- *Alfie Fripp was the longest serving British POW. He spent almost 6 years in 12 different German camps! While in Stalag Luft III in Poland in 1944, he helped 76 other POWs escape.*

JAPAN

Japan's harsh treatment of its prisoners was a sore point long after the war ended. In total, about 140,000 Allied prisoners were captured, held in camps, and forced to work in coal mines, shipyards, and factories. Disease and starvation were a constant threat in these camps, and thousands died as a result. Slave labor of up to 12 hours a day and a poor diet contributed to a staggering death rate in these camps spread across China, Burma, Korea, and other Asian countries.

The Bataan Death March forced around 80,000 POWs to walk 60 miles to the nearest camp. Many died on the way. Others faced indescribable torture and even had to suffer as medical experiments and target practice. One prisoner's body parts were cut off while he was alive, so his captors could see the effect!

The death rate was 27% compared to the low figure of around 4% in German and Italian camps. One of the reasons may have been because the Japanese saw surrender as a dishonorable act preferring to commit suicide rather than be taken captive. They saw it as their job to make these *weak* soldiers suffer for their shame.

AMAZING FACTS

- *Desperate for food, James "Ringer" Edwards, a POW in a Japanese camp, killed a cow to feed his fellow prisoners, but he was caught, and his punishment was to be crucified on a tree using barbed wire for 63 hours. Ringer survived!*

RUSSIA

Stalin always thought that Russia would need 4 million POWs for forced labor to rebuild cities that had been destroyed. Most of these were German soldiers, but the rest were citizens of captured countries, and were made to reconstruct dams, railroads, factories, and other structures.

Conditions in the 240 different camps were not good. As a German POW said, "At first, we had to load two train cars with wood during one work shift, then the norm was increased to three cars. We were forced to work 16 hours a day, on Sundays and holidays, also. We returned to the camp at nine or ten o'clock in the evening, but often at midnight. We received watery soup, and fell asleep, so the next day at five in the morning we would go to work again".

Food was the biggest issue for prisoners as rations were small, and starvation caused many deaths. An estimated 580,000 Germans died while in prison camps.

AMAZING FACTS

- *Repatriation is the moving back of prisoners to their own country and making sure that they are adequately taken care of. Because there were so many German POWs (2 million), it took almost five years until the last had been properly sent back.*

AMERICA

More than 400,000 Axis prisoners were kept in the United States where camps were set up in rural areas. Many were sent to farms or factories as there was such a shortage of workers at that time.

Life in the camps was sometimes better than their home life, and they received food, facilities, and treatment that was so good, one prisoner described it as a "golden cage". They could buy certain luxuries with the money they earned. There were hardly any escapes, and most POWs were happy to help America in the war cause.

AMAZING FACTS

- *American girls fell in love with many POWs kept in the United States, especially the Italians, but they were not allowed to marry them. After the war, they were given legal documents to get married in Italy, then come back with their husbands to America.*

BRITAIN

During the war, over 400,000 POWs from Italy, Germany, and Ukraine were kept in camps in Britain. There were hardly any escapes as most were content with the treatment they received while being held prisoner. They received the same rations as the ground troops and were paid for work they did.

Others were given the chance to work outside the camps, attending local churches, joining football teams, and becoming as much a part of the community as possible.

AMAZING FACTS

- *Some German officers were kept in luxury rather than a camp, so they would let down their guard while their conversations were monitored allowing the British to learn about the Holocaust, Hitler, and V2 rockets.*
- *24,000 German POWs remained in Britain after the war. The most famous was Bert Trautman who became famous as a goalkeeper for Manchester City Football Club in 1949 and went on to play for 15 years.*

FAMOUS POW'S PRISON ESCAPES

Where there's a prison, there will always be an escape, or somebody trying to get out! In WW2, there were plenty of stories of failed attempts, and those that were so daring and cunning that they succeeded.

The Wooden Horse

Oliver Philpot was part of a group of four men that used a wooden vaulting horse to escape from Stalag Luft III in 1943. The wooden horse was for the men to exercise, but Philpot and his men used the hollow of it to dig an elaborate tunnel from the middle of the grounds to the outside of the fence. Every day they covered the hole, and scattered the extra sand as they walked, so guards would not notice what they were doing.

Collecting fake identity papers and a compass, Philpot escaped with his group on October 29. He made it all the way to Sweden.

The Great Escape

Also from Stalag Luft III, Jimmy James and a group of men began digging three tunnels for 80 men to escape – the tunnels were named Tom, Dick and Harry! One of the tunnels was discovered, but the men continued with the others until March 25, 1944, when 80 men crawled through. Only three made it home. The remainder were all recaptured and 50 of them were murdered on Hitler's orders.

Eichstatt Tunnel

Mike Scott and 65 others escaped in June 1943 using a tunnel from the toilets up a hill to a village chicken coop. Over 50,000 police and guards were dispatched to find the missing men. After two weeks, most of the men were recaptured and sent to Colditz, a notorious castle prison.

Escape from Colditz

Lieutenant Airey Neave was the first British officer to make a successful escape from Colditz, one of the most famous POW camps. Colditz Castle, in eastern Germany, was built high on the slope of a hill and the Germans believed it was escape-proof. Throughout the war, they sent their most difficult POWs there. Airey Neave was sent there in May 1941 after escaping from his previous camp.

On January 5, 1942, Neave and a Dutch officer managed to get into the German guardhouse. Disguised as German officers, they walked out past sentries through a gate, across a park and over the wall. Wearing civilian clothes, they crossed into neutral Switzerland. On returning to the UK, Neave was employed by MI6 to help and advise other evaders and escapers, where he was codenamed 'Saturday'.

9

VICTORY CELEBRATIONS AND WHAT HAPPENED NEXT

VICTORY CELEBRATIONS

Imagine the joy people must have felt after 6 years of war, hardship and so much killing and destruction! Victory in Europe (VE) Day in Britain in was a time of immense happiness, relief, and celebration.

On May 8, 1945, people all across Britain erupted into jubilant celebrations as news spread that Germany had surrendered. The atmosphere was electric, with streets filled with cheering crowds, waving flags, and spontaneous dancing. Even the future Queen Elizabeth (then Princess Elizabeth) disguised herself and joined the celebrating crowds.

Crowds celebrating in London, Britain

In cities, towns, and villages, street parties sprang up. People decorated their homes and streets with flags, banners, and bunting. Tables were set up with food and drinks, and neighbors came together to share in the festivities.

Church bells rang out in celebration, and there were parades and processions featuring marching bands, military units, and veterans. People of all ages joined in, from young children to the elderly, united in their joy at the end of years of hardship and sacrifice.

Bonfires were lit, symbolizing the end of darkness and the dawn of a new era of peace. Firework displays illuminated the night sky, adding to the sense of excitement and celebration.

Winston Churchill, British Prime Minister, waving to the crowd in London

Amidst the revelry, there were also moments of reflection and sadness, as people remembered loved ones who had lost their lives during the war. But overall, VE Day was a time of overwhelming happiness and gratitude, as the nation came together to celebrate the hard-won victory and look forward to a brighter future.

And remember, the war in Pacific continued for some months after the Allied victory in Europe!

AMAZING FACTS

- *Food was rationed in Britain in 1940 as food was in short supply. This included sugar, meat, bacon and cheese. Although the war ended in 1945, rationing didn't finally*

end until 1954! Huge crowds gathered at shops when the rationing of sweets ended in 1953!
- *In 1946, to save fabric, swimming costumes had to be made 10% smaller – manufacturers simply removed the middle bit, and invented the bikini!*

Normandy Gravesite

What came next?

Many cities were left in ruins after the war. More than 70% of Germany's houses were gone as were 70,000 Soviet villages. Countries and their borders changed. Those nations that had been under German or Japanese rule had to be re-established. Orphans needed families. There was little food anywhere in Europe, and people starved. They had no homes, and the newly restored nations of Czechoslovakia pushed 3 million Germans from their borders, Poland did the same with over 1 million. Refugees by the thousands looked for places to stay.

German refugees wait in Berlin's Anhalter Station in 1945. Refugees are carrying their few belongings, as they stand behind a rope and double strand of barbed wire.

The Allies governed Germany until 1949, to help rebuild the country, and put in place a new German Government. The Marshall Plan provided billions of dollars of money for reconstruction. Germany was divided into two parts - East Germany was put under Russian control and West Germany was controlled by the Allies.

Austria was occupied by the Allies and only gained independence in 1955.

Japan was stripped of its army and overseen by the Allies who setup a 'no war' rule for the Japanese government, promising never again to use war to settle arguments.

But it was Russia that gained the most in the upheaval. Most of the countries they had swarmed across to reach Hitler, such as Ukraine, they simply held onto, swallowing them up into the new, expanded Soviet Union. This set up a new battle in the world, between democracy in the west, and communism in the east, with the United States and USSR (the new Russian federation) becoming superpowers.

AMAZING FACTS

- *Hiroo Onoda, a Japanese officer, never surrendered after the war and held his position in the Philippines until he was formally relieved of duty in 1974!*

Society

Massive changes occurred within each country as cities swelled with many people moving from the countryside. Women's roles in work and society also changed for the better, as they had played a large part in the war effort in factories and shown they could do the same jobs as men. With most of the men at war, it had been up to them to maintain farms, factories, and industry. As a result, women's rights began to be noticed, and in France and Italy, they were given the chance to vote for the first time.

Woman war worker checks 1,000 lb. bomb cases loaded with explosives. Firestone Tire and Rubber Co., Omaha, Nebraska. May 1943

One of the most significant outcomes of WW2 was the number of babies being born as soldiers returned from war and people were feeling more hopeful and excited about the future. In the US, between 1946 and 1964, just over 4 million new babies were born every year.

Racism had shown its ugly head in Germany with the Holocaust, and it was a reality that had to be dealt with, not just with Jews, but amongst those of color and different ethnic groups. In the United States, although the military was segregated during WW2, President Truman abolished it in the military. It took much longer for the whole country to scrap all segregation laws.

THE UNITED NATIONS

In 1945, the United Nations was created by 51 countries, as a place where they could talk and work out their differences, without going to war. The leaders from these countries wanted to make sure that the world could be a safer and more peaceful place for everyone.

It also led to the formation of the World Health Organization (WHO) to cope with the aftermath of the war as well as disease and illnesses going forward.

THE COLD WAR

Probably the most significant outcome of WW2 was the start of a new conflict. On February 9, Joseph Stalin of Russia gave a speech in which he declared that war between the East and West was inevitable.

On March 5, 1946, Winston Churchill coined the term "Cold War," warning *"From Stettin in the Baltic to Trieste in the Adriatic, an iron curtain has descended across the continent,"* and called for a strengthening of Anglo-American ties as well as *"a new unity in Europe from which no nation should be permanently outcast".*

With a full war between the new superpowers out of the question because of the threat of nuclear weapons, other means of gaining the upper hand were followed leading to subversion, espionage, and backing wars in other smaller countries. The Cold War was an intense stand-off between the United States and USSR that came close to full war during the Cuban Missile Crisis in 1962.

With the eastern parts of Europe such as Latvia, Hungary, Ukraine, Romania, dragged into an Eastern Bloc under Soviet rule, it was clear that there would be no agreement between western democracy and eastern communism. The Olympic Games and other sports events became a new battleground as each side fought for supremacy. The Cold War would last for 45 years until communism in Russia collapsed.

CONCLUSION

An event of the magnitude of WW2 cannot easily be forgotten or ignored. The effects and memories are like scars that may heal on the outside, once cities are rebuilt and society carries on, but the damage and horror that people had to endure can never fully be washed away.

Many may have risen to the occasion inspiring acts of heroism, bravery, and courage, but it also brought out the worst in nations. Fascism, racism, and greed for power steered thousands of people to commit terrible acts of savagery against fellow humans, even genocide. There was suffering on both sides - the winners and the losers. The Allies may have been victorious, but at what cost?

History is there as a teacher to help us learn which mistakes we should never repeat. The threat of war, genocide, and racism has not disappeared because a treaty was signed.

They are very real issues that can raise their heads again. If we are to learn from WW2, then it is to take note of what took place, the good and the bad.

We too can stand against those things that have ravaged the world. It all starts with tolerance and understanding, love and acceptance—for every color, creed, religion, ethnicity, and personality! War can never be the answer, even if it's one that's as small as in your own home!

> *"The greatest victory is that which requires no battle."*
>
> — SUN TZU FROM THE *ART OF WAR*

Congratulations! If you have read this far, you have achieved the final goal! But it's not all about reaching the end, it's about the journey to get there, and what we learn along the way. If you enjoyed this ride through WW2 with me, there's always another journey.

Look out for more history books, and sign up to my email list for more updates at james-burrows.com. And if you enjoyed my book, please leave me a review on Amazon!

ABOUT THE AUTHOR

James is an armchair military expert, developing an early interest in military history from stories told by his Grandfathers, one of whom was a POW spending 4 years in a camp in Poland, and even his Great-Grandfather, who fought at the Somme.

Whether writing about WW2, Roman Emperors or Alexander the Great, James hopes to spark a healthy curiosity and love for history in today's young people.

When not working or spending time with his wife and children, James can be found walking his two beautiful black labradors in the local countryside, pondering ideas for his next book.

www.ingramcontent.com/pod-product-compliance
Lightning Source LLC
Chambersburg PA
CBHW072055110526
44590CB00018B/3188